I-SEARCH FOR SUCCESS

A How-To-Do-It Manual
For Connecting the I-Search
Process With Standards,
Assessment, and
Evidence-Based Practice

Donna Duncan and
Laura Lockhart

HOW-TO-DO-IT MANUALS
FOR LIBRARIANS

NUMBER 136

NEAL–SCHUMAN PUBLISHERS, INC.
New York, London

Published by Neal-Schuman Publishers, Inc.
100 William Street, Suite 2004
New York, NY 10038

Library of Congress Cataloging-in-Publication Data

Duncan, Donna
I-search for success: a how-to-do-it manual for connecting the I-search process with standards, assessment, and evidence-based practice / Donna Duncan, Laura Lockhart.
        p. cm. — (How-to-do-it manuals for librarians ; no. 136)
    Includes bibliographical references and index.
    ISBN 1-55570-510-3 (alk. paper)
    1. Education—Standards—United States. 2. Educational evaluation—United States. 3. Curriculum planning—United States. 4. Education—Aims and objectives—United States. I. Lockhart, Laura. II. Title. III. How-to-do-it manuals for libraries; no. 136.

LB3060.83.D86 2005
379.1'58—dc22   2004054665

DEDICATION

To Bob, who has understood this writing process as none other could and who has supported and loved us through it, and to Laura, for being willing to juggle her busy life one more time in order to coauthor another book that will help teachers and librarians teach and children learn.

Donna Duncan

To Jordan, who has supported and encouraged us on yet another project, and to my Mom, for having the courage and commitment to share the vision of creating meaningful and exciting learning experiences for children.

Laura Lockhart

TABLE OF CONTENTS

LIST OF LESSONS

LIST OF FIGURES

FOREWORD

I-Search for Success is a significant addition to our profession and to our understanding of how librarians, teachers and children collaborate. From the 1970's to the present, library curriculum has evolved from the teaching of library skills to the teaching of information skills to the teaching of information literacy.

Library skills emphasized location and access. During library instruction, students learned how books were organized in the library. In 1979, Marcia J. Bates[1] outlined 29 search tactics in four categories: monitoring, file-structure, search-formulation, and term tactics. Since that time, library science professionals have developed a number of information literacy models with various degrees of success. This was followed in 1981 with the *British Library Research Model* using nine steps for students to ask beginning with "What do I need to do?" and ending with "What have I accomplished?" Similar to this was Gawith's *Action Learning Model*[2] condensing the process to six steps.

The introduction of *Information Skills Across the Curriculum*[3] by Ann Irving in 1985, highlighted the dual role of the teacher and library media specialist in the process. In 1988, Stripling and Pitts published *Brainstorms and Blueprints: Teaching Library Research as a Thinking Process*[4]. Their taxonomy included Recalling, Explaining, Analyzing, Challenging, Transforming, and Synthesizing. A significant breakthrough began in 1988, when Carol Collier Kuhlthau[5] wrote her dissertation on the *Information Seeking Process (ISP)*. This and her subsequent work focused attention on the students' affective experiences during research. Most importantly, Kuhlthau conducted meaningful research on students that formed the basis for subsequent models.

The most commercially successful of the emerging models was the Big 6 put forward in 1990 by Mike Eisenberg and Bob Berkowitz[6], which reduced the process to a simplistic and easy to follow format. In the same year in Alberta, the Provincial Ministry of Education developed a model known as *Focus on Research*.[7] This process-based model focused on the process of research as well as the product where the primary emphasis was not given to product. Many others contributed their own version of a model including Alice Yucht[8], V. Rankin[9], George and Garner[10], Grover and Fox[11], Washington Library Media Association[12], Vermont Educational Media Association[13], the Information Network for Ohio Schools[14], Charles and Jean Schulz[15], Trevor Bond[16], Deubert and Grey-Smith[17], Jamie McKenzie[18], plus others. One of the best-known models presented was *Pathways to Knowledge* by Pappas and Tepe[19] who stressed the fact that their model was non-linear. Also, David Loertscher who suggested the *Circular Model*, advocating time for the student to read, view, listen, and sort it all out.[20]

However, the most influential work contributing directly to this book was the work of Joyce and Tallman who published *Making the Writing and Research Connection with the I-Search Process*[21]. The aim of the *I-Search* model was to engage students in meaningful problem solving and help them determine their personal approach to research. One aspect of this model that differs from the others is the topic choice. The topic should be something useful to the student. In other words, research should not be something done only because a teacher or librarian assigns it to the student. The information of the search should be something of use and/or interest to the student. The I-Search is a student-centered approach to the research process. Librarians and partner teachers serve as facilitators of the process—modeling, coaching, and scaffolding the process. Students keep a learning log throughout the research unit monitoring what they learned and how they learned it. They reflect on the techniques and strategies that worked best for them and predict how they will use these strategies in future research assignments. The emphasis on metacognition helps students transfer the process to new learning situations.

With *I-Search for Success*, Duncan and Lockhart have taken this to a new level that is instantly user friendly. It goes well beyond their previous book to provide librarians and teachers with the necessary tools to assist students in the research process.

Barbara Stein Martin, Professor
University of North Texas
School of Library and Information Sciences

NOTES

1. Bates, Marcia J. 1979. "Information Search Tactics." *Journal of the American Society for Information Science* 30, no. 7: 205-14.

2. Gawith, Gwen. 2003. "Re: Action Learning and 3 Doors Models." (23 October 2003).

3. Irving, Ann. 1985. *Study and Information Skills across the Curriculum*. London: Heineman.

4. Stripling, Barbara K., and Judy M. Pitts. 1988. Brainstorms and Blueprints. Englewood, CO: Libraries Unlimited.

5. Kuhlthau, Carol Collier. 1993. *Seeking Meaning: A Process Approach to Library and Information Services*. Norwood, UK: Ablex.

   ———. *Teaching the Library Research Process*. 1994. London: Scarecrow Press.

6. Eisenberg, Michael B., and Robert E. Berkowitz. 1990. *Information Problem-Solving: The Big Six Skills Approach to Library & Information Skills Instruction*. Norwood, UK: Ablex.

7. Dianne Oberg. *Teaching the Research Process for Discovery and Personal Growth*. International Federation of Library Associations and Institutions. Available: http://www.ifla.org/IV/ifla65/papers/078-119e.htm (20 January 2004).

8. Yucht, Alice H. 1997. *Flip It! An Information Skills Strategy for Student Researchers*. Worthington, OH: Linworth Publishing.

9. Rankin, V. 1992. "Rx: Task Analysis or Relief for the Major Discomforts of Research Assignments." *School Library Journal* 38, no. 11: 29-32

10. *Research Analysis Communication*. Caroline County Public Schools. Available: http://cep.cl.k12.md.us/RAC/RACSite/RACHome.html (20 January 2004).

11. Grover, Robert, Carol Fox, and Jacqueline McMahon Lakin. 2001. *The Handy* 5. Lanham, MD: Scarecrow Press.

12. *Wlma and Ospi Essential Skills for Information Literacy*. Washington Library Media Association. Available: http://www.wlma.org/Instruction/wlmaospibenchmarks.htm (20 January 2004).

13. *Using Vermont's Framework of Standards and Learning Opportunities: Information Literacy for Vermont Students: A Planning Guide*. Vermont Department of Education/Vermont Educational Media Association. Available: http://www.vita-learn.org/anesu/infolit/guide.htm (20 January 2004).

14. *Infohio Dialogue Model for Information Literacy Skills*. INFOhio - The Information Network for Ohio Schools. Available http://www.infohio.org/id/dialogue.html (20 January 2004).

15. *The Research Process*. Sonoma State University. Available: http://libweb.sonoma.edu/assitance/research/default.html (20 January 2004).

16. Bond, Trevor. "Re: Sauce Model." *Sauce for Research & Problem Solving* ICT in NZ. Available: http://ictnz.com/SAUCE.htm#ictintegration (20 January 2004).

17. *Info Trek: Your Guide through the Information Maze*. Curtin University of Technology. Available: http://library.curtin.edu.au/ infotrekk/ (20 January 2004).

18. McKenzie, Jamie. 2000. *Beyond Technology: Questioning, Research and the Information Literate School*. Bellingham: FNO Press.

19. Pappas, Marjorie L., and Ann E. Tepe. 2002. *Pathways to Knowledge and Inquiry Learning*. Greenwood Village: Libraries Unlimited.

20. David V. Loertscher. 2000. *Taxonomies of the School Library Media Program*, 2nd ed. San Jose, CA: Hi Willow Research & Publishing.

21. Joyce, Marilyn Z., and Julie I. Tallman. 1997. *Making the Writing and Research Connection with the I-Search Process*. New York: Neal-Schuman.

PREFACE

In our last book, *I-Search, You Search, We All Learn to Research* (2000), we shared our experiences and findings from using the I-Search method in elementary school. The I-Search process works because children learn best when they are given opportunities for exploration and to make decisions about their learning. We explained how this process empowers students, brings out their curiosity and love of learning, and lays a foundation for building a community of lifelong learners. Our first book showed readers "how to" teach this method to students from start to finish. *I-Search for Success* provides even more instruction and tips for sharing the process with your students, but it also demonstrates how it can be effectively incorporated into your curriculum to meet and exceed the new mandated standards.

We wrote *I-Search for Success* because we found that the utilization of this method not only fans the flame of student and teacher interest, but also enhances achievement on today's new state-mandated assessments. We have spent our careers in a high-stakes test state, Texas, which has had state assessment since the mid-eighties. The most effective and successful teachers have utilized strategies and methods that help their students learn to think and solve information problems as opposed to teaching them "to the test." Integrating instruction for information problem-solving into the curriculum helps students achieve and surpass state educational goals because these integrated elements provide students the opportunity to master the standards, to increase their academic achievement, and to become lifelong learners.

By now, many of us are familiar with the I-Search process. It is rooted in research, but unlike traditional research, which typically occurs in school, university, and lab settings, this process is applicable to everyday needs inside and outside the educational setting. Ken Macrorie, author of *The I-Search Paper*, described it as a practice of a person who conducts a search to find out something he needs to know for his own life and who writes the story of his adventure (1988). It is an inquiry-based process that compels students to move away from the traditional research report format in which they restate old information (Macrorie, 1988). We base the I-Search process on five action questions:

QUESTION! What do we want to know?

EXPLORE! Where can we find the information?

CREATE! How will we understand and record the information?

PRESENT! How will we show what we learned?

JUDGE! How will we know we did a good job?

I-Search for Success presents concept-based units that will help teachers and librarians:

- collaborate for success;
- integrate evidence-based practice into the classroom;
- achieve standards;
- provide authentic assessment; and
- prepare students for standardized tests.

It incorporates research-based instructional strategies including the "nine instructional strategies that have a high probability of enhancing student achievement for all students in all subject areas at all grade levels" as identified by Marzano, Pickering, and Pollock (2001). In addition, these units integrate Bloom's Taxonomy, the information literacy standards from the American Association of School Librarians (AASL) and the Association for Educational Communications and Technology (AECT), as well as differentiated instruction strategies for teaching reading and for writing informational text.

Lessons in *I-Search for Success* incorporate the reading and writing objectives that are regularly tested. Increasingly, state assessments require students to read, analyze, and interpret informational text. It is imperative that today's students have access to instruction that provides them opportunities to develop information literacy skills. These skills are not only necessary to prepare students to succeed on the test, but will also prove invaluable in a real world that values literacy and communication skills.

COMPONENTS

THE I-SEARCH UNIT INSTRUCTION MANUAL

Part I, "Making the I-Search Connection," includes two chapters. Chapter 1, "Connecting with Standards-Based I-Search Units," presents evidence-based practice, standards, tests, authentic assessment, and student achievement to this innovative research process. Chapter 2, "Connecting with Collaborative Partnerships," covers many of the topics you will need to share and work on with faculty, administrators, and your school community, including creating collaborative action research projects, financing, showing evidence, and communicating.

Part II, "Connecting I-Search the Five Questions of I-Search Learning," contains chapters that outline the searching and reporting process: "What Do We Want to Know?," "Where Can We Find the Information?", "How Will We Understand and Record the Information We Find?," "How Will We Show What We Learned?," and "How Will We Know We Did a Good Job?." These chapters utilize instruction and advice, feature more than 20 sample lessons, assessment rubrics, sample journal portfolios, self-evaluation guidelines, grade sheets, and unit assessments to ensure the proper delivery and execution of the I-Search process to your students.

As a whole, Parts I and II:

- identify the connections in the standards that provide the basis for concept-based I-Search units;
- explain questioning strategies that incorporate Bloom's Taxonomy and the information literacy standards;
- offer pre-search lessons that address reading standards and tested objectives;
- outline the writing process that incorporates the writing standards, "write traits," and tested objectives;
- supply information-location skills lessons;
- provide multiple lists of Web sites;
- develop authentic assessment ideas for rubrics, portfolios, and other grading tools; and

• showcase twenty developmentally appropriate lessons aligned with the McREL (Mid-continent Research for Education and Learning) standards and benchmarks and with the AASL/AECT Information Literacy Standards.

Part III, "Connecting I-Search with Teaching Tools," includes the following:

A. The Teacher/Team/Library Media Specialist Collaborative Planning Guide

B. The Student I-Search Journal

C. Model I-Search Unit: Our National Heritage—This Land Is Our Land

D. Staff Development PowerPoint Presentation

Sections A, B, and D appear on the CD-ROM for easy reproduction and customization.

We hope that teachers, LMS, administrators, curriculum personnel, and graduate students will find that *I-Search for Success* facilitates learning and increases student success. We define success as helping to make certain that students attain goals on state standardized tests, become prepared for the next grade level, develop a foundation for an increasingly technological world of work, and are given a voice in what they learn and what they want to be! Collaboratively, teachers, LMS, administrators and parents can help all students succeed!

Please share your success with us at banddduncan@msn.com and LELockhart@aol.com.

ACKNOWLEDGMENTS

We would like to thank our families and friends for their support and concern as this project has evolved. Our husbands, Jordan and Bob, have once again been patient and willing to assume additional family responsibilities in order to give us time to work on the book. Our grandchildren, Mallory and Duncan, continue to inspire us to write books that will help them develop life skills that will contribute to their social well-being.

We appreciate, too, the many teachers, librarians, and administrators with whom we have worked during the past five years as we have designed units and implemented the I-Search process on multiple campuses and in a variety of districts. The librarians in the Mesquite Independent School District deserve special recognition; they embraced the idea of a collaborative partnership with their faculties and went the extra mile time and time again to design units, juggle schedules, and teach alongside their teachers in order to provide positive learning opportunities for their students.

We want to thank Jane Ann Thompson, former library consultant for the Texas Region Ten Education Service Center, who encouraged us to incorporate the standardized test objectives into the I-Search Process. We also want to thank Barbara Martin for continuing to encourage us to write about our experiences with the I-Search process from the prospective of teacher, librarian, and administrator.

In addition we would like to thank our editors, Charles Harmon and Michael Kelley. Charles encouraged us to write a second book and has shepherded us through the process. Michael, in his kind and persistent manner, has made writing this second book a fascinating and educational experience.

Lastly, we want to thank Ken Macrorie for writing the original *I-Search Paper.* His wisdom and foresight has paved the way for personalizing the research process and has provided students and teachers the opportunity to become excited about finding answers to their questions. As others have said, he put the "search" back in "research."

MAKING THE I-SEARCH CONNECTION

1 CONNECTING WITH STANDARDS-BASED I-SEARCH UNITS

INTRODUCTION

The I-Search Unit provides opportunities for students to develop questions, research the answers, record their findings, and illustrate their learning through products while reflecting on and evaluating their learning. This information problem-solving model is very similar to the one we used in *I-Search, You Search, We All Learn to Research*. It is based on five questions aligned with the higher order thinking skills of Bloom's Taxonomy. The model also aligns with the AASL/AECT Information Literacy Standards, McREL's Standards and Benchmarks, differentiated curriculum strategies, as well as other scientifically based instructional strategies. These important connections result in powerful learning opportunities and experiences for students. (See Figure 1-1.)

REFLECT EVIDENCE-BASED PRACTICE

An incredible number of ideas, activities, and teaching strategies are available for educators. They are challenged to sort through the multitude of options to determine which will best meet student needs, increase achievement, and prepare them for the future. The Department of Education changed the way these decisions are made with the passage in 2001 of the No Child Left Behind Act. United States Secretary of Education, Rod Paige, has said, "A central concept in the No Child Left Behind Act of 2001 is that federal funds should support programs and strategies that are backed by scientifically based research." (Paige, 2002: www.ed.gov/pressreleases/11-2002/11182002b.html:12213012002) Grover J. (Russ) Whitehurst, assistant secretary of Educational Research and Improvement for the Department of Education, defines evidence-based education as "the integration of professional wisdom with the best available empirical evidence in making decisions about how to deliver instruction." (n.p.) He observes that:

I-Search Action Plan	Bloom's Taxonomy	Differentiated Curriculum Strategies	Information Literacy Standards	McREL Standards/Benchmarks Language Arts—Level II
What do we want to know?	Knowledge	Choice of topic Student interest Goal setting Varied questioning strategies Multiple intelligences Independent study	Standard 4: Student pursues information related to personal interests Standard 9: Student participates effectively in groups to pursue and generate information	Standard 4: Gathers and uses information for research purposes Standard 7: Uses reading skills and strategies to understand and interpret a variety of informational texts
Where can we find the information?	Comprehension	Access to wide range of materials and technologies Varying organizers Varied homework Small group instruction	Standards 2, 3, 9 Standard 1: Student accesses information efficiently and effectively	Standards 1 and 4 Standard 5: Uses the general skills and strategies of the reading process Standard 8: Uses listening and speaking strategies for different purposes
How will we understand and record the information we find?	Application and Analysis	Higher level thinking Process differentiation Graphic organizers Complex instruction	Standards 1, 4 Standard 8: Student practices ethical behavior in regard to information and information technology Standard 3: Student uses information accurately and creatively	Standard 1: Uses the general skills and strategies of the writing process Standard 4 Standard 5 Standard 7
How will we show what we learned?	Synthesis	Varied homework Multiple intelligence Tiered products Student interest	Standard 3 Standard 5: Student appreciates creative expressions/information Standard 7: Student recognizes importance of information to democratic society	Standard 1 Standard 2: Uses the stylistic and rhetorical aspects of writing Standard 4 Standard 7 Standard 8
How will we know we did a good job?	Evaluation	Ongoing assessment Teacher/student developed rubrics Portfolios Activity Checklist	Standard 2: Student evaluates information critically and competently Standard 6: Student strives for excellence in information seeking	

Taken from *Taxonomy of Educational Objectives* by Benjamin Bloom, 1984; *Leadership for Differentiating Schools and Classrooms* by Carol Ann Tomlinson and Susan Demirsky Allen, 2000; *Information Power: Building Partnerships for Learning* by American Association of School Librarians and Association for Educational Communication and Technology. Copyright ©1998 American Library Association and Association for Educational Communications and Technology. Reprinted by permission of the American Library Association; Copyright 2000 McREL, Mid-continent Research for Education and Learning, 2550 S. Parker Road, Suite 500, Aurora, CO 80014, 303/337-0990 (www.mcrel.org/standards-benchmarks)

Figure 1-1. I-Search Unit Connections

Evidence-Based Education's major components are empirical evidence and professional wisdom. Empirical evidence includes scientifically based research and objective measures. Scientifically based research is composed of practice and programs while objective measures include benchmarks and local data. The other major component of evidence-based education is professional wisdom that includes personal experience and consensus views. (www.ed.gov/print/admins/tchrqual/evidence/whitehurst.html) See Figure 1-2.

A press release from the U. S. Department of Education on April 24, 2002, announced that the Department of Education and the Council for Excellence in Government's Coalition for Evidence-Based Policy would collaborate on a new initiative that will:

explore how the department can most effectively advance evidence-based approaches to federal education policy. This initiative is designed to help the department achieve the goal of transforming education into an evidence-based field as outlined in the department's recently released strategic plan. The initiative will also advance the key principle in the No Child Left Behind Act of 2001: that federal funds should support programs and strategies that are based on scientifically based research. (Department of Education, Press Release, April 24, 2002)

This is a new world for educators. A world in which scientifically based instructional innovation will be necessary for the purpose of increasing student academic achievement.

School librarians are positioned to be collaborative partners in this process. Ross Todd, associate professor at Rutgers University, has become an outspoken advocate for the relevance of school librarians in the area of evidence-based practice. In the November 2001 issue of *Orana,* he summarized the components of evidence-based practice as identifying learning needs, developing instructional strategies, and evaluating those strategies in terms of the differences it makes to student learning. He goes on to write that evidence-based practice "might be in the form of statistics, or stories, or documented case studies, or analyses of reflective student interviews, student portfolios and reflective journals, or a range of other feedback processes. It does not need to be complicated but manageable, and clear." (Todd, 2001: 17) It is our goal that *I-Search for Success* be "manageable and clear." It is a resource guide that provides scientifically based instructional strategies

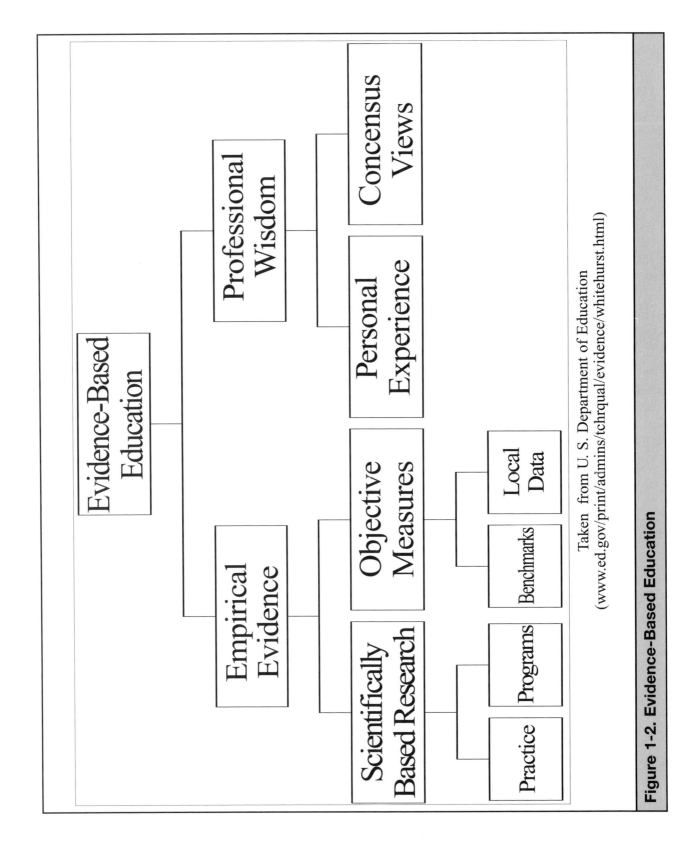

Taken from U. S. Department of Education
(www.ed.gov/print/admins/tchrqual/evidence/whitehurst.html)

Figure 1-2. Evidence-Based Education

evaluated with authentic assessments that will indicate increased student learning when implemented correctly.

One example of scientifically based instructional strategies is the meta-analysis study done by the researchers at Mid-continent Research for Education and Learning (McREL). They analyzed selected research studies that could be used by teachers in K–12 classrooms and identified nine instructional strategies that are detailed in *Classroom Instruction that Works: Research-Based Strategies for Increasing Student Achievement* by Marzano, Pickering, and Pollock. They maintain that the nine strategies they identify "have a high probability of enhancing student achievement for all students in all subject areas at all grade levels." (Marzano, Pickering, and Pollock, 2001: 7) We have integrated those nine strategies into the 20 lessons presented in this book. See Figure 1-3.

The I-Search Unit also addresses the challenge of providing effective instruction for mixed-ability classroom populations. Differentiated curriculum strategies are integrated throughout the instructional process of the unit as students are given choices of products, work with graphic organizers, set goals, develop questions, work in groups, and are assessed with rubrics and portfolios. In the article, "Reconcilable Differences: Standards-Based Teaching and Differentiation," Carol Ann Tomlinson maintains, "Standards-based instruction and differentiated learning can be compatible approaches in today's classrooms." (Tomlinson, 2000: 6) I-Search Units are an example of this compatibility. See Figure 1-1, Column 3.

Finally, cooperative learning activities are integrated throughout the instructional process. Reflection questions and group processes are used to develop metacognitive skills and enrich the classroom community. Both cooperative learning and group processing are confirmed to "lead to greater retention of subject matter and academic achievement." (Gibbs, 2001) Gibbs writes:

> Throughout the years, CenterSource Systems trainers have been helping teachers define three types of refection questions (1) about the content (facts and concepts) of a lesson; (2) about the collaborative social and constructive thinking skills used by students within their tribes; and (3) about the personal learning and meaning that a lesson had for the students. Reflection questions were emphasized as a way to develop metacognition (learning about our learning) and responsibility among students to improve their learning groups (tribes). Empirical studies confirm that the time spent with students on

Marzano, Pickering, and Pollock's Instructional Strategies	Standards-Based I-Search Unit Instructional Activities
Identifying similarities and differences	• Careful Reading Strategies—Lesson 4 • Context Clues/Vocabulary Development—Lesson 5 • Fact/Opinion—Lesson 12
Summarizing and note taking	• Research Workshop Chapter 5 • Search Log—Chapter 5 • Keyword Searches—Lesson 6 • Using E-Sheets/Internet Lesson 7 • Interviewing Experts—Lesson 8 • Taking Notes—Lesson 9 • Summarizing Note Sheets—Lesson 13 • Summary Boards—Lesson 14 • Summarizing the Search—Lesson 18
Reinforcing effort and providing recognition	• Rubrics (products/performance)—Chapter 7 • Process Writing—Lesson 19 • Product Presentations—Lesson 20 • Unit Celebration—Chapter 1
Homework and practice	• I-Search Project Contract—Chapter 3 • Careful Reader Strategies—Lesson 4 • Research Workshop—Chapter 5 • Interviewing Experts—Lesson 8 • Product Development—Lesson 20
Nonlinguistic representation	• Making Predictions—Lesson10 • Reciprocal Teaching—Lesson 11 • Drawing Conclusions—Lesson 15
Cues, questions, and advance organizers	• Developing I-Search Questions—Lesson 2 • I-Search Action Plan—Chapter 1 • Fact and Opinion—Lesson 10 • Summarizing the Search—Lesson 18 • Note Sheets—Lesson 9 • Making Predictions—Lesson 10
Cooperative learning	• Research Workshop—Chapter 5 • Writing Workshop—Lesson 19 • Making Presentations—Lesson 20
Setting objectives and providing feedback	• Student I-Search Journal—Chapter 1 • I-Search Paper, Presentations, and Product Rubrics—Chapter 7 • I-Search Journal Portfolio—Chapter 7
Generating and testing hypothesis	• Independent I-Search project
Taken from *Classroom Instruction that Works: Research-Based Strategies for Increasing Student Achievement* by Marzano, Pickering, Pollock, 2001, ASCD (www.ascd.org)	

Figure 1-3. Research-Based Strategies for Increasing Student Achievement

"group processing" also leads to the greater retention of subject matter and academic achievement. (Gibbs, 2001: 403)

INTEGRATE THE STANDARDS

Robert Marzano, one of the foremost authorities of the standards movement, has compared education standards to standards used in other areas of society such as those required in bridge building or food production. Standards are "that level of knowledge or skill we expect students to reach in a specific subject matter." (Marzano, 2003: http://webserver2.ascd.org/tutorials/standards/ques1.html)

Nationally, multiple fields of study such as math, fine arts, language arts, history, and social studies began to develop standards in the late eighties and early nineties. McREL (Mid-continent Research for Education and Learning) began systematically collecting, reviewing, and analyzing national and state curriculum documents in all subject areas in the fall of 1990, and from this they published their first technical report, *The Systematic Identification and Articulation of Content Standards and Benchmarks: An Illustration Using Mathematics.* A second edition published in 1995 was *Content Knowledge: A Compendium of Standards and Benchmarks for K–12 Education.* Since then, they have published a third edition and are working on a fourth. These editions can be accessed at www.mcrel.org. The McREL Language Arts Standards and Benchmarks–Level II are used in each of the 20 lessons of the I-Search Unit. (See Figure 1-1, Column 5.) Social Studies standards/benchmarks for grades K–4 from the fourth online edition of McREL's *Content Knowledge* are used in the sample unit in Part III-C as well as in lesson one in Chapter 3.

The nine information literacy standards located in *Information Power: Building Partnerships for Learning* are also a part of the standards movement "designed to guide and support library media specialists" efforts in the three main areas of learning and teaching, information access, and program administration." The "Levels of Proficiency" within the book are based on a variety of relevant sources and are designed to reflect the levels of learning outlined in Bloom's taxonomy. These levels of learning "show how students can build from a beginning awareness of information literacy to a more complex understanding." (*Information Power: Building Partnerships for Learning,* 1998: xi) (See Figure 1-4.) Figure 1-1, Column 4 illustrates how the information literacy standards compare to the I-Search Action Plan, Bloom's Taxonomy, differentiated curriculum strategies, and

The Nine Information Literacy Standards for Student Learning

Information Literacy

Standard 1: The student who is information literate accesses information efficiently and effectively.

Standard 2: The student who is information literate evaluates information critically and competently.

Standard 3: The student who is information literate uses information accurately and creatively.

Independent Learning

Standard 4: The student who is an independent learner is information literate and pursues information related to personal interests.

Standard 5: The student who is an independent learner is information literate and appreciates literature and other creative expressions of information.

Standard 6: The student who is an independent learner is information literate and strives for excellence in information seeking and knowledge generation.

Social Responsibility

Standard 7: The student who contributes positively to the learning community and to society is information literate and recognizes the importance of information to a democratic society.

Standard 8: The student who contributes positively to the learning community and to society is information literate and practices ethical behavior in regard to information and information technology.

Standard 9: The student who contributes positively to the learning community and to society is information literate and participates effectively in groups to pursue and generate information.

Information Power: Building Partnerships for Learning by American Association of School Librarians and Association for Educational Communication and Technology. Copyright ©1998 American Library Association and Association for Educational Communications and Technology. Reprinted by permission of the American Library Association.

Figure 1-4. The Nine Information Literacy Standards for Student Learning

McREL's Language Arts Standards Level V, all of which have varying degrees of complexity and are integrated into the I-Search Unit.

There is a wide range of thought and feeling toward the standards. It has become clear that parents, the general public, and a lot of teachers feel positively about them. In their article, "Standards: Here Today, Here Tomorrow," Matthew Gandal and Jennifer Vranek review three opinion surveys that "paint an unmistakable picture of support for this direction of school improvement." The surveys conducted for the Business Roundtable, The Public Agenda, and the January 2001 issue of *Education Week* all indicated public support for the standards. Gandal and Vranek maintain:

> The public will continue to support standards so long as the students who reach them are prepared to succeed in the next grade, in college, and in meaningful careers. These are the tangible outcomes that parents want for their children. (Gandal and Vranek, 2001: 8–10)

The world in which we live will not reward workers with only minimum skills. Effective workers need to productively use resources, interpersonal skills, and information technology, as well as to understand social, organizational, and technological systems. (Learning a Living: A Blueprint for High Performance, A SCANS Report for America 2000, 1992: xiv) As the career expectations of children increase, the support of standards will continue to grow.

There are multiple standards in each discipline in each of the grade levels. As a result, "in many classrooms, students 'cover' lots of facts, vocabulary words, names, dates, and rules. Unfortunately, they also forget much of what they 'learn' as they leave that information behind and move on to another topic or lesson." (Tomlinson, 2001: 74)

A meaningful alternative to teaching such as this is "concept-based teaching." Concept-based teaching promotes teacher clarity about common learning goals, gives a clear and powerful focus of instruction for struggling students, provides a platform for meaningful extension of learning for advanced learners, and crosses cultures to connect with students of varied backgrounds. Concept-based curriculum is challenging to create and vastly worth the effort. (Tomlinson, 2000: 91)

I-Search units are based on the concepts of standards that are the unit focus. For example standards for a kindergarten science unit might include the seasons of the year. An I-Search Unit on Change would reflect the concept of the seasons and provide the "powerful focus of instruction and platform for meaningful extension of learning" that Tomlinson describes. (Tomlinson, 2000: 91)

INCORPORATE STANDARDIZED TESTS AND AUTHENTIC ASSESSMENT

Pressure on educators for accountability has been building since 1983 when the report, *A Nation at Risk*, was first published. The report deemed America's public school system a failure and a threat to our economic survival. Accountability has increased with the passage of the No Child Left Behind Act of 2001 (NCLB). With NCLB educators must now make annual progress or face serious sanctions that could result in teachers and administrators being replaced and schools ultimately being turned over to private management or state control. (Dallas Morning News, October 5, 2003)

Pressure of that magnitude can paralyze the best of educators and pressure them to "teach to the test," which limits student educational experiences. James Popham, in the March 2001 issue of *Educational Leadership,* expressed his concern about this problem in his article, "Teaching to the Test?" He asks, "In an era of high-stakes and high-stress testing how do we ensure that classroom instruction does not give way to inappropriate teaching?" (Popham, 2001: 16) He describes item teaching as test questions driving the daily activities and curriculum. In contrast to item teaching, he described curriculum teaching as teaching that will elevate students' scores on high-stakes tests and their mastery of the knowledge or skills on which the test items are based. (Popham, 2001: 17)

Curriculum teaching includes assessing students in order to make instructional decisions and monitor progress. In his article "Can School Media Programs Help Raise Standardized Test Scores?," Doug Johnson observes:

> From my experience here in Minnesota, I can't truthfully say that high-stakes basic skills testing has been all bad. In fact, I've liked what has happened in our district since kids that can't demonstrate they can read, compute or write at a minimal level aren't being allowed to graduate. Suddenly these invisible children whom we've quietly passed on from grade to grade until passing them out of the system have become glaringly visible. As a result, our district has magically found some resources to provide remedial instruction, summer school and early reading intervention programs. It really appears more kids in our district are becoming functionally literate because of

the pressures resulting from these tests. (Johnson, 2000: 27)

Johnson continues with the following reminder:

> Businesses have been asking schools to produce graduates not just with basic skills, but also more importantly with the ability to solve problems, to communicate, to collaborate, to be organized and to be creative. The development of new kinds of tools to measure student learning and to aggregate individual data from those measurements that will show school effectiveness is probably the most important thing we as educators can be doing right now. (Johnson, 2000: 28)

Johnson's analysis of today's educational climate underscores our charge to integrate, differentiate, and analyze instruction for ultimate student success. Through this process we can provide evidence of student growth and achievement.

Students need multiple and varied opportunities to share what they have learned in order to provide that evidence of growth and achievement. We were reminded of this one afternoon while visiting a school in a low socioeconomic area. A third-grade class was in the library doing research on space. The students were reading and taking notes from information books. Engrossed in one of the books was a little fellow who was considered "Limited English Proficient." He was having difficulty taking notes but when asked to explain what he was reading, he very clearly explained in a child's version the "big bang theory" using the pictures in the book.

In his book, *The Rubrics Way: Using Multiple Intelligences to Assess Understanding*, David Lazear discusses "multimodal assessments as a means to ensure that all students are given fair ways to demonstrate their understanding of the various subject areas and concepts in the school curriculum." (Lazear, 1998: 16) We agree that students need multiple opportunities with different modalities to demonstrate their competence.

Authentic assessments found in this book include an I-Search journal portfolio and rubrics based on the multiple intelligences. In addition, there are 28 activities within the 20 lessons that may be assessed as the unit progresses. These allow the teacher and library media specialist (LMS) to view the progress of students throughout the unit. A Standards-Based Grade Sheet lists these activities and provides a place for the grades in Chapter 7. A personal evaluation form for students and a collaborative unit assessment for teachers and LMS are included as well.

I-Search Units also incorporate the reading comprehension and writing skills most likely to be tested on state assessments. These include reading skills such as context clues, prediction, fact and opinion, sequencing, inference, and summarization. Writing lessons include the six writing traits of ideas, organization, voice, word choice, sentence fluency, and conventions. These skills taught in the context of an I-Search Unit using multiple types of informational text "increase student motivation, build important comprehension skills, and lay the groundwork for students to grow into confident, purposeful readers." (Duke, 2004: 43)

INCREASE STUDENT ACHIEVEMENT

As parents and grandparents we want more for our children and grandchildren than high scores on the state-mandated tests. Doug Johnson summed it up when he wrote:

> As a parent, yes, I want to know my son's standardized test scores, but I also want to see projects that require higher-level thinking skills, view a critiqued portfolio of his work that shows growth, read reports of his ability to work collaboratively, review evidence of his ability to self-assess his work, and watch him use his skills to make a thoughtful difference in society. (Johnson, 2000: 28)

That is what we all want for our students and we can provide those experiences in spite of the pressure to focus instruction on test preparation. A student who illustrates this and who stands out in our memory is a young man in the fourth grade who had failed the state reading test as a third grader. He was a bundle of nerves and fearful that he would fail the test again. His parents were teachers in the district, and that contributed even more to his anxiety. The project-centered classroom of his fourth-grade year gave him multiple opportunities to read, write, research, produce products, and present his ideas. These opportunities helped him develop confidence as a reader, writer, and thinker. He became confident of his ability and when it came time for the state test, not only did he pass it, but he also performed at a high level and, more importantly, became a reader!

Readers become thinkers and that skill will extend throughout their lives. A former student who has since graduated from high school and college and now owns an interior-design business in a large city is a prolific reader who daily uses the thinking skills she developed in school. She looks back on the classes where she was given the opportunity to ask questions, research the answers, and develop and present products about her findings as foundational in the work she now does. The opportunity to solve real-world problems early in life has provided a foundation for problem solving as an adult.

Though Andrew Young did not know these students, he spoke of their needs in his address to the Association for Supervision and Curriculum Development in San Francisco, California, in March 2003, when he reminded educators that "students are struggling with the changes in the world, and it is important to give them a voice. As we pull out of those young people the best of their thinking, the best of their courage, as we develop their confidence ... then we will have people who are inspired with a passion for learning." (Quindlen, 2003: 1)

2 CONNECTING WITH COLLABORATIVE PARTNERSHIPS

Many campus administrators are concerned that their students are motivated and excited about learning and that their teachers develop the skills needed to integrate state-assessed instructional and test objectives into meaningful instruction. This focus on the achievement of students on their campus is not uncommon. As a result, administrators and teachers tend to consider new instructional programs if other campuses similar in size and socioeconomic level have used the program and have been successful. Ross Todd affirms this observation:

> Principals, teachers, parents want to hear local success, local improvement; they want to know how their students in particular are benefiting, not how others are doing. Local outcomes matter; local improvements are noticed, listened to, indeed sought after, underscoring the critical importance of teacher-librarians being engaged in evidence-based practice that shows that their role in the learning goals of the school makes a difference. (Todd, 2001: 15)

He explains further:

> Evidence-based practice focuses on two things. Firstly, it is the conscientious, explicit and judicious use of current best evidence in making decisions about the performance of the role. It is about using research evidence, coupled with personal professional expertise and reasoning to implement learning interventions that are effective. … Secondly, evidence-based practice is about ensuring that day-to-day efforts put some focus on effective evaluation that gathers meaningful and systematic evidence on dimensions of teaching and learning that matter to the school and its support community, evidences that clearly convey that learning outcomes are continuing to improve. (Todd, 2001: 15)

Instruction such as this takes time to plan and is strengthened through collaborative partnerships between teachers and the LMS.

I-Search for Success is an information-literacy curriculum resource guide that can be used in a variety of ways by teachers, teams, and the LMS to develop collaborative lessons, units, and even action research projects that will increase student motivation and provide evidence of student achievement.

DEVELOP INSTRUCTIONAL PARTNERSHIPS

The instructional goal for a LMS is to develop collaborative teaching partnerships with his/her faculty. Lance, Rodney, and Hamilton-Pennell explained in "How School Librarians Help Kids Achieve Standards: The Second Colorado Study":

> Test scores rise in both elementary and middle schools as library media specialists and teachers work together. In addition, scores also increase with the amount of time library media specialists spend as in-service trainers of other teachers, acquainting them with the rapidly changing world of information. (Lance, Rodney, and Hamilton-Pennell, 2000: 1)

Teacher and LMS collaborative partnerships may be as simple as the LMS working with a single teacher to develop a library lesson that relates to the unit of study in the classroom or as complex as working with multiple teams and developing an information literacy curriculum integrated into standards-based units for all grade levels that are implemented throughout the year.

ONE TEACHER/ONE CLASS

There are twenty lessons in *I-Search for Success* some of which can be taught in isolation from the I-Search process. For example, the Wonderful Words activity in Lesson 5 became a favorite of teachers who used it in the Collaborative Action Research Project we conducted. Others include Careful Reading Strategies in Lesson 4, Key Word Searches in Lesson 6, Making Predictions in Lesson 10, Reciprocal Teaching in Lesson 11, and Fact and Opinion/Web-site Evaluation in Lesson 12. These lessons are rich in literature and technology and will add interest and variety to a teacher's lesson plans as well as provide support for standardized test preparation and information literacy. Use them with teachers who come to you and want help with just one lesson to support a test skill or objective or a classroom unit.

ONE TEACHER/ONE UNIT

One teacher and the LMS may collaborate on a unit. They both need to be comfortable with the constructivist method of teaching, in which students are given an opportunity to develop questions and find individual meaning, as well as to solve problems with information resources and make real-world connections to their learning. Demonstrate that reading and writing standardized test objectives can be documented as being integrated into the research process. The unit will last approximately six weeks if one 45-minute session is devoted to it daily. This time will vary depending on the number of lessons included and whether more time per day is spent on the unit. Integration of science or social studies, reading, writing, research, and technology standards in the unit justifies spending the time normally spent on those subjects on the unit daily. In that case, the unit could be taught in considerably less time than six weeks.

The model unit, "Our National Heritage—This Land Is Our Land," may be used. The level is fourth grade but it can be modified for older students or simplified for younger ones. The student I-Search Journal is also a key component of the unit. It helps the teacher and LMS guide the students through the research process. Everyone begins together and ends together. Collaboratively teaching the unit from start to finish provides both the teacher and LMS a picture of the I-Search process. The first time through the research process is sometimes difficult and frustrating as illustrated in the Kuhlthau Model of the Information Search Process. (See Figure 3-4.) Second and third units become easier as everyone involved (teachers, students, parents, and LMS) becomes comfortable with the process and knows what to expect. Collaboratively teaching the unit from start to finish at least one time is essential before attempting to work as a grade-level team.

ONE TEAM/ONE UNIT

Principal support and team ownership are the prerequisites for collaborating with a grade-level team to plan an I-Search Unit. In addition the LMS needs to understand and be committed to the instructional process, have a handle on staff development, and be very organized. The following steps are good places for the LMS to start when planning a unit:

- Use the PowerPoint presentation in Part III-D to provide an overview of the unit process for the team.
- Take time to discuss the lessons as you go through the presentation and point out that they are based on the standards and integrated with an information problem-solving model.
- Highlight the lessons that specifically address the standardized test objectives that they are required to teach.
- Schedule the unit or units that the team wishes to teach during the year.
- Spend time planning the unit in depth about six weeks in advance using the Collaborative Planning Guide found in Part III-A of this book. Some principals hire substitutes for a day or an afternoon in order to allow time for their teachers to plan. Other administrators have asked parents to cover the classes. Planning this far ahead gives everyone time to process the unit concepts and start gathering materials.
- A final planning session should occur a week or two before the unit begins in order to tie up loose ends and make last-minute decisions. Informal planning has been occurring during the six weeks since the first formal planning session.
- The next four to six weeks will be busy and oftentimes hectic as you juggle the research needs of several classes at the same time. Teachers often get frustrated as they adjust their schedules with others but the payoff is worth it as everyone sees the level of instruction rising and the learning opportunities increase for their students.
- The Unit Celebration is the last joint instructional effort of the team. Keep it simple. The focus should be on the student presentations. Invite parents and administrators to be a part of their students' success.
- Be sure to evaluate the unit after it is completed. Use the Teacher/Library Media Specialist Evaluation of a Collaboratively Taught Unit Form in Chapter 7 and keep the meeting brief. Serve refreshments, invite your administrator, celebrate your successes, and correct your mistakes. File the unit and unit resources for the following year.

• Share your success with other teams and fellow LMS on other campuses and in other districts.

MULTIPLE TEAMS/MULTIPLE UNITS

Working with multiple teams to teach multiple units is very similar to working with one team. It just takes more time, more commitment, and more organization on the part of the LMS. A couple of things need to be done differently when working with multiple teams:

• Staff Development—Provide the unit overview using the PowerPoint (Part III-D) with all the teams at one time. This is especially effective during a two- or three-day summer staff-development session. The first day can provide an overview of the unit process and time for teams to decide which unit/s they wish to teach. The second (and third) day(s) can be devoted to scheduling the unit/s and initial unit planning.

• Scheduling Units—Each team decides which unit or units they would like to teach and when they would like to teach it/them. A successful scheduling technique we have used displays the months of the school year from a poster-size calendar around the room. Each team decides which unit/s they plan to teach and posts sticky notes on the dates when they would like to teach it/them. Scheduling problems will emerge and participants will need to negotiate in order to satisfy the needs of all the teams. The LMS then creates a curriculum calendar and gives copies to the team members and administration.

• Planning Early—Planning this early gives everyone time to think about the unit(s) and decide how to modify them. In addition, it gives the LMS time to acquire materials to support the multiple units.

• Campus Curriculum Fair—A Campus Curriculum or Technology Fair can be planned by the really brave of heart for an end-of-the-year celebration. One campus presented an example of this idea when multiple teams taught integrated units throughout the year. They decided to highlight the technology projects that were used in their units. The third-grade team on that campus had taught a unit on jungle animals. Their students were responsible for doing research on the jungle animal of their choice. They had the opportunity to use both print and online encyclopedias as well as other resources to do their research. Each student was responsible for developing a fact and opinion slide about his or her animal. The slides were then put together for a class PowerPoint presentation. Students were as excited about their research and projects at the end of the year as they were when they presented them at their Unit Celebration. A celebration such as this gives everyone in the school an opportunity to see what other classes and teams have done. It is also a great time to invite parents, community members, central administration, and the board of trustees.

SHOW THE EVIDENCE

Todd reports that Oberg in "Demonstrating That School Libraries Improve Student Achievement" (2001) identified a range of evidence-based practices. Action research was one example. Oberg explained "action research projects provide real, creative, and collaborative opportunities for teacher-librarians to initiate and document learning improvements." (Todd, 2001: 17)

Action research projects are effective tools to use to integrate staff development, concept-based learning as illustrated by I-Search Units, and authentic assessment in order to demonstrate increased student achievement. Collaborative Action Research projects incorporate both empirical evidence and professional wisdom and "involve a wide array of methods derived from both the quantitative and qualitative domains." (Sagor, 1993: 9)

Richard Sagor has written an easy-to-read book on collaborative action research for the Association for Supervision and Curriculum Development (ASCD). In his book, *How to Conduct Collaborative Action Research,* he explains: "Action research ... is conducted by people who want to do something to improve their own situation. ... Action researchers undertake a study because they want to know whether they can do something in a better way. Sagor's five-step Collaborative Action Research Project includes problem formulation, data collection, data analysis, reporting the results, and action planning (replicating the plan). In addition, the Development and Dissemination School Initiative Web site at (www.alliance.brown.edu/dnd/ar_websites.shtml) lists Action Research Web sites by Richard Sagor.

Using this five-step process as a foundation and consulting colleagues in other districts and the Region Service Center, we developed a Collaborative Action Research Project to determine if integrating the tested reading objectives of the state mandated test into I-Search Units at the third-grade level would help increase student achievement in four test schools. Three of the schools were located in one district and a fourth in another district. The results were positive in three schools and nonconclusive in the fourth school because of insufficient data. Though the study was small and the results not fully conclusive, it did open the door for additional studies that might reveal consistent trends of increased student achievement when authentic assessment and evidence-based practice are integrated in an I-Search Unit or other similar evidence-based practice. (See Figure 2-1.)

Information Literacy Collaborative Action Research Project

Problem Formulation:

- Identify the issues six months to a year before project implementation. Discuss the project with your administrator/s. Decide who will be involved in the project. Determine which classes will be the test groups and which will be the control group if doing a Randomized Study.*

- Formulate with the project participants a question to address (e.g., how does collaborative teaching of the standards integrated with information literacy and the standardized test objectives increase student achievement?)

- Schedule the initial two-day training.

- Two to three months before the training meet with the staff development personnel and develop the two-day training program. Use the I-Search for Success PowerPoint and the unit example, "This Land Is Our Land," as the focus for the training. Start acquiring materials for the training.

- Conduct the initial training one to two months before school starts. Teachers in the test groups should be trained. They may be in grade-level teams if the study is being held in multiple schools. If the study is on one campus, some of the classes in the same grade level may be randomly selected as either test or control groups.

- The training should include an overview of the I-Search process using the unit example on the first day.

- Time to discuss the units that will be planned and taught and actual planning for the first unit should be provided on the second day of training.

- A project calendar should indicate when the benchmark tests occur, the units will be taught, and the actual standardized test given. The first unit should be taught after the first benchmark, the second unit after the second benchmark and before the actual test.

(continued on next page)

Figure 2-1. Information Literacy Collaborative Action Research Project

Data Collection:
- Collects cognitive data on the benchmarks and actual test for both the test and control groups. Collected data throughout the year as the tests are given.
- Collects affective data from participant surveys in regard to the effectiveness of the program and teacher/LMS/student evaluations of the I-Search units.

Data Analysis:
- Test results are disaggregated when the final results are available. Charts and graphs should be created to indicate the results of both the test and control groups.
- Surveys and evaluations should be analyzed for problems and successes.

Reporting the Results:
- Share the results with your campus, district, region and nationally through such forums as the American Association of School Librarians, LM_NET, and "Project Achievement" at (www .davidl.org).

Action Planning (Replicate the Plan)
- Use your findings to replicate the study in other areas of your school and district.

*Randomized Study—Meaningful measures of achievement to compare several schools that used a given program with several carefully matched control schools that did not. (Slavin, 2003: 13)

Collaborative Action Research Plan outline taken from *How to Conduct Collaborative Action Research* by Richard Sagor, Association for Supervision and Curriculum Development, Alexandria, Virginia, 1992.

Figure 2-1. Information Literacy Collaborative Action Research Project, continued

FIND THE MONEY

Evidence-based practices such as these are examples of "innovative" instructional programs that can be used to find grant money. Pressure to increase student achievement is happening at the same time that budgets are being cut. "The need to find grant money to fund instructional programs and professional development is increasing. The ability to write grants has become a critical survival skill." (Knickelbine, 2003: 12) Scott Knickelbine, has written:

> Current federal grant programs almost universally emphasize the development of model programs to identify best instructional practices. That means that your grant proposal for books and materials may stand a better chance if it's written in the context of an instructional pilot project. (Knickelbine, 2003: 12)

Figure 2-2 lists specific grants that are available to fund evidence-based instructional programs such as the one described in this book. The more aware the LMS is of curriculum issues and how they can be integrated with information literacy and increase student achievement the more likely they are to be successful in their search for grant money.

Professional Development Grants

Federal Grants:

- IDEA Grants:
  (www.ed.gov/offices/OSERS/SASA/cepprogresp.html)

- Reading First State Grants:
  (www.ed.gov/offices/OESE/readingfirst/grant.html)

- Improving Literacy Through School Libraries:
  (www.ed.gov/offices/OESE/LSL/index.html)

- Innovative Programs:
  (www.ed.gov/offices/OESE/SST/ieps.html)

Private Grants:

- Cingular Wireless:
  (www.cingular.com/about/charitable_contribution_guidelines)

- NEA Foundation for the Improvement of Education:
  (www.nfie.org/programs/grantguides.htm)

- The Coca-Cola Foundation:
  (www2.coca-cola.com/citizenship/foundation_guidelines.html)

- The Starbucks Foundation:
  (www.starbucks.com/aboutus/grantinfo.asp)

Stay current and visit The Foundation Center: (fdncenter.org)

Taken from, "The Money Hunt," by Scott Knickelbine, *School Library Journal*, (Curriculum Connection) October 2003, p. 12.

Figure 2-2. Professional Development Grants

SHARE THE JOURNEY

School library programs are a part of the transition of public education. Old solutions no longer work. We're in need of new and dynamic instructional programs that will facilitate this transition. Ross Todd reminds us that:

> Evidence-based practice certainly requires effort, but the skills needed to engage in this practice stem directly from the information-literacy processes that we preach. What's important is that the gathered evidence highlights how the librarian plays a crucial role in boosting student achievement, in shaping important attitudes and values, in contributing to the development of self-esteem, and in creating a more effective learning environment. (Todd, 2003: 54)

Presenting or sharing our findings is an important part of the information-literacy process. We provide opportunities for our students to share their findings. We need to do the same for ourselves. David Loertscher has developed a national initiative to collect and present evidence at the local level that links school library programs to student achievement. Information on "Project Achievement" may be found at (www.davidvl.org).

John Naisbitt in *Megatrends: Ten New Directions Transforming Our Lives* wrote: "Trends, like horses, are easier to ride in the direction they are already going. When you make a decision that is compatible with the overarching trend, the trend helps you along. You may decide to buck the trend, but it is still helpful to know it is there." (Naisbitt, 1982: 9) The trend in education is increasing accountability for the standards and increased student achievement on the state-mandated tests. These are tremendously powerful trends. Educators are challenged to capture the energy within these trends and funnel them into creative educational experiences for their students.

Our invitation to you is that you follow these trends through the next five chapters that represent the "five questions that connect learning." These five chapters contain twenty lessons that will guide you and your students through the information problem solving process with side trips to examine reading and writing opportunities that will enhance the adventure. Share the journey with others and with us as together we increase student achievement and their involvement in learning.

II CONNECTING THE FIVE QUESTIONS OF I-SEARCH LEARNING

3 WHAT DO WE WANT TO KNOW?

PLAN THE UNIT

Plan the Unit	Two Planning Sessions 4–6 weeks before unit	Teacher/Team/LMS Responsible

• Establish the Timeline
• Unit at a Glance
• Choose the Standards
• Develop the Unit Concepts
• Construct Student I-Search Journals
• Determine Unit Assessment

Chapters 3 through 6 are a resource guide to help plan and develop I-Search Units. The five research questions that tie the units together are further connected with 20 easy-to-follow lessons. In addition, there is a Collaborative Planning Guide template, a student I-Search Journal template, a sample I-Search Unit, and a staff development PowerPoint overview in Part III. The planning guide, I-Search Journal, and PowerPoint are also on an enclosed CD-ROM. The focus of this process is to provide student opportunities to develop questions of personal interest within the context of the standards-based I-Search Units. (See Figure 3-1.)

ESTABLISH THE TIMELINE

Calendars and planners are consulted to determine the dates for planning, teaching, culminating, celebrating, and evaluating the unit. Finding a time that is good for all participants is sometimes hard. Scheduling a major research unit just before the holidays or the end of school in order to keep the students busy during a difficult instructional

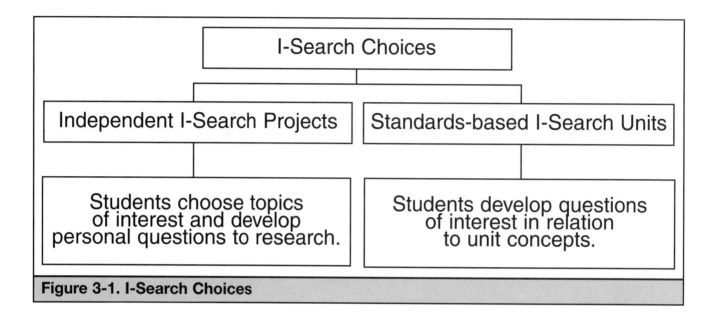

Figure 3-1. I-Search Choices

time will only result in frustrated students, teachers, LMS, and parents. Experience has taught us that the most productive units are scheduled during the fall semester before the winter holidays. Before spring break during the spring semester is also an effective time for a unit. The variety of activities and the reading and writing objectives addressed in an I-Search Unit enhance test preparation. It gives students an opportunity to think creatively and at a high level. A unit timeline helps establish when the major activities of the units will take place. (See Figure 3-2).

UNIT AT A GLANCE

Another helpful planning tool is "Unit at a Glance." (See Figure 3-3). This aid lists the number of 30- to 45- and 45- to 60-minute sessions it normally takes to teach the 20 lessons and the person responsible for instruction. The unit can last anywhere from four to six weeks depending on the number of lessons taught and the skill level of the students. It is important to give students time to process and internalize information. Carol Kuhlthau's "Model of the Information Search Process" illustrates the need for students to spend time processing their feelings, thoughts, and actions when they are involved in a research project. (See Figure 3-4.) Consulting the Unit Timeline, Unit at a Glance, and Information Search Process charts should give you a realistic picture of the time commitment needed for a unit.

UNIT TIMELINE

ACTIVITY	DATE
Planning	
Teaching	
Unit Celebration	

Figure 3-2. Unit Timeline

LESSONS	ESTIMATED TIME	PERSON RESPONSIBLE
What do we want to know? Chapter 3		
Unit Planning	1 to 2 planning sessions—4–6 weeks before unit	T and LMS
L1: Unit introduction	4-5 LL	T and LMS
L2: Developing questions	2-3 SS	T or LMS
L3: I-Search action planner	1 SS	T or LMS
Where can we find the information? Chapter 4		
L4: Careful reader strategies	1 SS	T or LMS
L5: Context clues/Vocabulary development	1 SS	LMS or T
L6: Key word searches	1 SS	LMS or T
L7: Reciprocal teaching	1 LL	T or LMS
L8: Interviewing experts	1 SS	T or LMS
How will we understand and record the information we find? Chapter 5		
L9: Take notes/Cite sources	1 LL	T or LMS
L10: Fact and opinion	1 SS	T or LMS
L11: Web Site evaluation	1 SS	LMS or T
L12: Research workshop	3-5 LL	LMS and T
L13: Summarize notes	1 SS	T and LMS
		T
How will we show what we learned? Chapter 6		
L14: Summary Boards	1 SS	T or LMS
L15: Draw conclusions	1 LL	T or LMS
L16: Develop main idea	1 SS	T or LMS
L17: List sources	1 SS	T or LMS
L18: Summarize search	1 LL	T or LMS
L19: Writing workshop	2-3 LL	T
L20: Products/Presentations/ Celebrations	4-5 LL	T and LMS
How will we know we did a good job? Chapter 7		
Student rubrics/Tests/Portfolios	1 SS	T
Unit assessments	1 SS	T and LMS

KEY

T=Teacher

LMS=Library Media Specialist

Position listed first should lead the activity.

SS (Short session)=30 to 45 minutes of lesson time

LL (Long lesson)=45 to 60 minutes of lesson time

Figure 3-3. Unit at a Glance

Stages	Task Initiation	Topic Selection	Prefocus Exploration	Focus Formulation	Information Collection	Search Closure	Start Writing
Feelings	uncertainty	optimism	confusion frustration doubt	clarity	sense of direction/ confidence	relief	satisfaction or dissatisfaction
Thoughts		ambiguity	ambiguity	ambiguity increase interest	specificity increase interest		
Actions		seeking	relevant	information	seeking	pertinent information	

Source: Kuhlthau, Carol Collier. (2004). *Seeking Meaning: A Process Approach to Library and Information Services*, 2nd ed., Westport, CT: Libraries Unlimited, 45.

Figure 3-4. Kuhlthau Model of the Information Search Process

CHOOSE THE STANDARDS

Most schools have curriculum maps that have been developed in response to state-mandated curriculum standards. These maps determine when specific standards/objectives are taught. The standards of most interest to students have the best chance of succeeding in an I-Search Unit. Consulting the LMS at this point is a good idea because he/she deals with all students and is aware of their interests.

The standards used in the unit example in Part III-C are the McREL Level II (Grades 3–4) History Standards and Benchmarks. We also used these standards throughout in Chapters 3, 4, 5, and 6. See Figure 3-5. In addition, the McREL Language Arts reading, writing, listening, and speaking standards/benchmarks are integrated in the 20 lessons in the unit.

DEVELOP UNIT CONCEPTS

Determining the concepts of the standards on which to focus is the next step. It is fairly common for this step to be skipped. An example of this occurred when a team of third-grade teachers and their LMS decided to teach a unit on biomes. The immediate idea was to let each of the students choose a biome to research. Upon examination of the standard, it was apparent that the concept was on the interdependence of plants and animals within the biome. For example, the desert tortoise is facing the threat of extinction because of the introduction of alien annual plants into the desert. (Berry, 1998) An I-Search question such as "What is killing the desert tortoise?" would be an interesting question for this unit. Students make emotional connections to their learning with questions such as these.

Determining Unit Concepts:

1. The collaborative team of teacher/s and LMS decides which standards to teach.

2. The facilitators analyze and web the standards selected for the unit to determine the concepts of the unit. See Figure 3-6.

3. The facilitators list the concepts. They are an indication of what information needs to be taught and researched. Some of the basic concepts can be covered in introductory lessons and throughout the unit during whole class lessons. See Figure 3-7 for an example of concepts for a unit on National Heritage.

McREL K-4 History Standard and Benchmarks (3rd ed.)

<u>Topic 4</u>—The History of Peoples of Many Cultures Around the World

<u>Standard 6</u>: Understands the folklore and other cultural contributions from various regions of the United States and how they helped to form a national heritage.

<u>Level II (Grades 3–4)</u>

<u>Benchmarks</u>:

1. Knows regional folk heroes, stories, or songs that have contributed to the development of the cultural history of the U. S. (e.g., Pecos Bill, Brer Rabbit, Paul Bunyan, Davey Crockett, John Henry, and Joe Magarac)
2. Understands how stories, legends, songs, ballads, games, and tall tales describe the environment, lifestyles, beliefs, and struggles of people in various regions of the country
3. Understands how arts, crafts, music, and language of people from a variety of regions long ago influenced the nation

© 2000 McREL, Mid-continent Research for Education and Learning, 2550 S. Parker Road, Suite 500, Aurora, CO 80014, (303) 337-0990 (www.mcrel.org/standards-benchmarks)

History Standards and Benchmarks, Level II (Grades 3-4) are used for the model unit. Language Arts Standards and Benchmarks, Level II (Grades 3-5) are used for the 20 lessons. These levels were chosen so they could be simplified for younger students and expanded for older students.

Figure 3-5. McREL K-4 History Standard and Benchmarks (3rd ed.)

4. The teachers, LMS, and students discuss the projects and possible student rubrics. Students will have the opportunity to develop questions of personal interest based on unit concepts in Lesson 2.

At this point the teacher/s and the LMS have chosen the topic for the unit and have reviewed the standards that need to be met. Decisions have been made about which concepts will be taught in the introductory activities and throughout the unit.

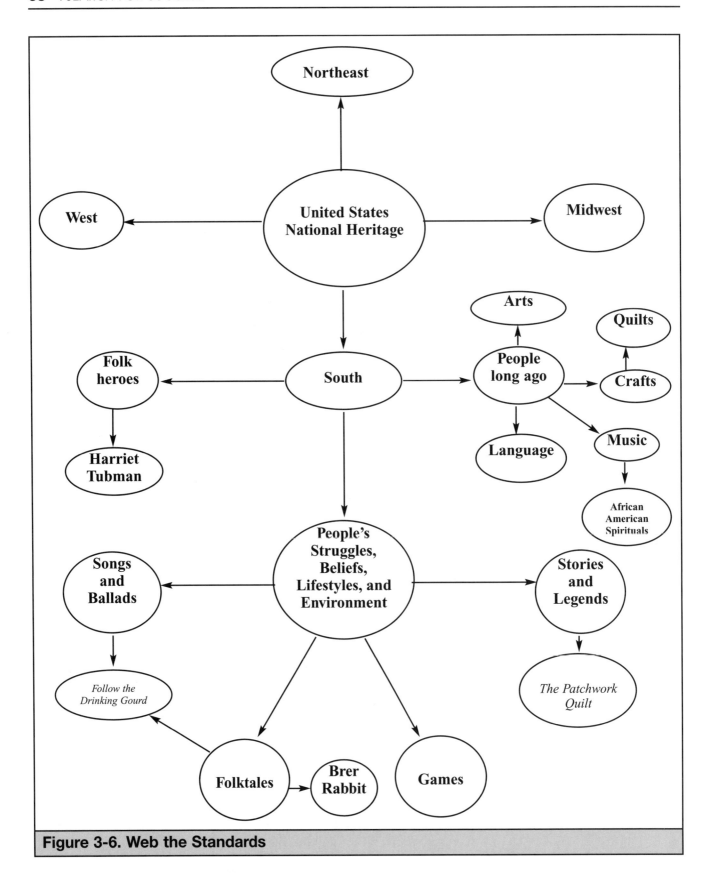

Figure 3-6. Web the Standards

UNIT CONCEPTS

- Culture influences our lives.

- People are different in the various regions of the United States. All regions have folk heroes who have contributed to the cultural history of the United States.

- Stories, legends, songs, ballads, games, and tall tales describe the environment, lifestyles, beliefs, and struggles of people in the various regions both today and long ago.

- Folklore contributions such as arts, crafts, music, and language of people from all the regions combine to form the national heritage.

Figure 3-7. Unit Concepts

The 20 lessons are structured for maximum student understanding and learning. Students are introduced to concepts and activities and have opportunities to see skills modeled and to participate in guided practice. They will also have opportunities to work with concepts and skills independently through group and individual practice. Many of the lessons and strategies presented in this book are ongoing and used before, during, and after the unit. We have attempted to integrate reading, writing, speaking, listening, and research skills in the unit in a manner that makes each skill meaningful and provides students opportunities to apply them.

CONSTRUCT STUDENT I-SEARCH JOURNALS

Experts such as Robin Fogarty, in her book, *The Mindful School: How to Teach for Metacognitive Reflection,* and Peter Elbow, the pioneer of Learning Logs as a metacognitive tool for students, both assert that the Learning Log is a viable tool for students as they accept more and more responsibility for their own learning (Elbow cited in Fogarty, 1994: 15).

The Student I-Search Journal is a key feature of this research process. Advanced preparation includes putting together an I-Search Journal for each student. A three-ring binder with pocket dividers lends itself to an I-Search Journal Portfolio. It's important to have the I-Search Journals ready for the students when the unit begins. You may want to modify the journal to meet the requirements of the unit you design and the level of your students.

DETERMINE UNIT ASSESSMENTS

It's good to start the I-Search Unit with the assessment in mind. Students need to know up front how grades are determined. Chapter 7 details the I-Search Unit assessment process and provides examples that can be adapted to specific units. The assessment types include rubrics, a research journal portfolio, checklists, personal evaluations, and a list of activities that are taught throughout the unit that assess the reading, writing, listening, and speaking standards and benchmarks. Decide in the beginning which assessments and evaluations will be used in the unit.

Chapter 3 Lessons
• Lesson 1: Unit Introduction—Parts 1, 2, 3, and 4
• Lesson 2: Develop Questions—Parts 1 and 2
• Lesson 3: I-Search Action Planner

Lesson 1 Parts 1, 2, 3, and 4	Unit Introduction	4–5 sessions	Teacher/Team/ LMS responsible

The unit introduction develops the knowledge base upon which students will build. It helps construct background knowledge and creates interest and the spirit of inquiry. Take time to build a solid foundation in order to insure a successful unit. Following are ideas and activities to consider when developing introductory activities.

Materials needed

- Posters, pictures, and artifacts that create an exciting atmosphere. Students should be able to observe, handle, and discuss the objects
- Video clips about the subject matter

- High-interest books (fiction and nonfiction) to read and discuss
- Poetry to read and share over the unit of study
- Students bring artifacts from home
- I-Search Journals for each student

Lesson Objective

The objective of lesson one is to introduce the unit to the students, create interest in the subject, tap prior knowledge, build background knowledge and fluency skills, introduce the I-Search Journal, and begin the process of determining what students will research.

Standards/Benchmarks

Content standards vary according to unit focus and content. See Figure 3-5 for an example of regional folklore standards.

McREL Standards/Benchmarks—Language Arts—4th ed.

- Standard 4: Gathers and uses information for research purposes.
  1. Uses a variety of strategies to plan research (e.g., identifies possible topic by brainstorming, listing questions, using idea webs; organizes prior knowledge about a topic; develops a course of action; determines necessary information).
- Standard 7: Uses reading skills and strategies to understand a variety of informational texts.
  1. Uses prior knowledge and experience to understand and respond to new information.

AASL/AECT Information Literacy Standards

- Standard 9: The student who contributes positively to the learning community and to society is information literate and participates effectively in groups to pursue and generate information.

Lesson 1: Part 1— Introductory Activities sample lesson	One to two 45–60-minute sessions	Teacher/Team/LMS

The focus of the sample unit in Part III-C is Our National Heritage. A unit such as this is a unit on the people of the United States. Choose from the following suggested introductory activities:

- The book, *People*, written and illustrated by Peter Spier, is a good book to illustrate this truth. Reading it to the class or sharing the video as an introductory activity would be a great way to help students start thinking about our national heritage being a result of "people (who) come in all sizes and shapes: tall, short, and in-between... ." (Spier, 1980: 2)

- Once it has been established that this unit is really a unit about people, it is then time to focus on the fact that it is a unit about people in the United States. A good book/video to use for this part of the introduction is *This Land is Your Land*, by Woody Guthrie. This is an illustrated ballad in book and video form that "takes the reader on a walk from coast to coast." (Blecher-Sall, Waddington, and Law, 2001: 69) Having a large United States map posted in the classroom will enhance the unit and this activity in particular.

- After getting an overview of the geography of the United States, spend time discussing the four regions that include the Northeast, South, Midwest, and West. (Buckley, 1997: 37)

- Now that you have your students thinking about people and their unique qualities in the various regions of the United States, it is time to think about how this forms the National Heritage. A quilt is a good analogy:

> Quilting is thus a symbol that provides a medium that allows for expression that is representative of its original beginnings as a houseware and art form—an inclusive and intermixed tradition comprised of varied backgrounds and cultures and histories. Quilting is a medium that can bring contrasting backgrounds together to create a new meaning from the intermixture of its contrasting influences. (Leigh, 2003: http://xroads.virginia.edu/~UG97/quilt)

There are multiple resources dealing with quilts. Display real quilts, show slides/videos about quilts, or share and discuss books such as The Patchwork Quilt, by Valerie Flournoy, to help students understand that we are all unique people with special gifts that add to the color and texture of our National Heritage. See the resource list in Part III-C for additional quilt resources.

> • The I-Search Journal is a key part of the I-Search process. It helps provide students with a sense of ownership and an awareness of the research process. Review the journal with your students when you distribute it. File the journals in the classroom and use them during research time.

The students have begun to build their knowledge base with the many activities of the unit introduction. It is now time to start helping them focus on topics that they would like to find out more about. Webbing project ideas, thinking about topic choices, skimming and scanning, and completing I-Search topic homework assignments help students make this decision.

Lesson 1: Part 2— Student Project Web	One to two 45–60-minute sessions	Teacher/Team/LMS support

Materials Needed

- United States map
- Overhead projector and dry-erase pens
- Transparency of Figure 3-8
- Blank project web
- I-Search Journal for each student

Lesson Objective

Students will have opportunities to brainstorm and web ideas for an I-Search project.

McREL and AASL/AECT Standards same as Lesson 1—Part 1

Guided Practice and Independent Work (Student Project Web)

Model the process in a think-aloud fashion so that the students will see what and how you are thinking. This encourages students to dig deeper into their own experiences and interests to find possible I-Search topics. The following is a step-by-step process that is used to help students work through this activity.

- Review the four regions of the United States. Students should choose one region to research.
- Discuss with students how the Project Web will help them focus on the topic they want to research for their I-Search project.
- Model for students by making the initial part of the web with the boxes that lists the cultural contributions. (See Figure 3-8.)

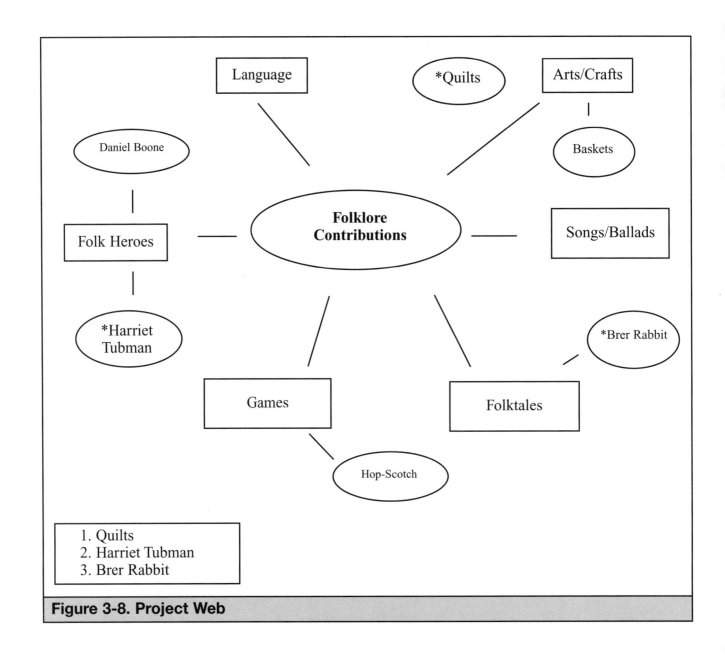

Figure 3-8. Project Web

- Create a second layer for each box with an oval that is a specific example of the cultural contribution. Students repeat the process. (See Figure 3-8.)

- Model choosing the top three topics in the ovals about which you would like to know more. Put a star by the top three. Students repeat the process.

- Rank the choices from number one to number three. List them at the bottom of the page. Students repeat the process.

- Share with students the reason for your decision. Have them turn to a friend and discuss their top three possible topics. Encourage them to give personal reasons for choosing each one.

Closure/Input/Reflection:

- Model writing on each possible topic. Read and think aloud. Have students write on their three topics. (See Figure 3-9.)

- The first two entries in the I-Search Journal are the Project Web (Figure 3-8) and Possible I-Search Topic sheets (Figure 3-9). After making the first two entries, each classroom stores them by groups/classes. Storing the I-Search Journals in groups/classes allows for easy access and avoids the problem of being lost.

- Go through each I-Search Journal after the first assignment to determine if it is complete. Check to see if students are on the right track and if they're beginning to think about meaningful topics that will carry them through the research.

- Respond to their work by encouraging and providing helpful suggestions. Write suggestions directly on the journal or on sticky notes. Also, make note of any student who may need a preliminary conference to get on the right track.

Possible I-Search Topics

My first choice of a topic is _____

because _____

_____ .

My second choice of a topic is _____

because _____

_____ .

My third choice of a topic is _____

because _____

_____ .

Figure 3-9. Possible I-Search Topics

Lesson 1: Part 3— Skimming and Scanning	One to two 45–60- minute sessions	LMS/Teacher/Team

Materials Needed
- Library Media Center (LMC)
- LRC Resources
- I-Search Journals

Lesson Objective
Students will have opportunities to skim and scan for resources for their top three I-Search topics.

McREL & AASL/AECT Standards same as Lesson 1—Part 1

Guided Practice and Independent Work

Students need opportunities to make an informed and well-thought-out decision about their I-Search topic. They need to explore various sources to get a feel for it. A skimming and scanning visit to the LMC gives them this opportunity. Allow 45 minutes to an hour in the LMC for each visit. The LMS may need to provide a brief orientation lesson depending on the experience of the students.

- Students are asked to search for sources on all three of their top choices.

- They are asked to think of answers to two questions while they are looking through the resources: Will there be enough information on the topic of my choice? Is the subject interesting?

- Encourage your students to look at pictures, captions, and bold and italicized print. Also, have them read titles, topic sentences, and the conclusions of paragraphs for the sources.

- Keep the atmosphere in the LMC relaxed, fun, and full of excitement. Students should be sharing, talking, and absorbing a little about each of their topics. This trip gives students the opportunity to make discoveries and become more responsible for their own learning as they build background knowledge. Building this background knowledge will help them develop higher-level questions.

Closure/Input/Reflection

- At the end of the first day, students reflect on their findings. This can be done on notebook paper and added to their I-Search Journals. Questions on which they reflect may include:

    1. Which topic had the most sources?
    2. Which topic seems to be the most interesting?
    3. What will be my goal for tomorrow?

- The I-Search Journals are reviewed after the first LMC trip to evaluate where the students are and to help them with any problem areas.

Second Day

- The following day is much like the day before. Students, however, are encouraged to review their I-Search Journal reflections from the previous day. This will help them be more directed and goal oriented for the day's work.

- At the conclusion of the second day, students will need to make a preliminary decision on their topic. On their Possible I-Search Topic sheets, students put a star by the topic they are most inclined to choose. They should choose a topic based on the availability of sources, but most importantly on their interest.

Lesson 1: Part 4— I-Search Topic Homework	1st session, 15–20 minutes, 2nd session, 30–45 minutes	Teacher/Team

Materials Needed

- Figure 3-10—I-Search Topic Homework for each student
- I-Search Journals for each student

Lesson Objective

Students will have opportunities to consult with their parent/guardian in regard to their I-Search topic and write an explanation of why they made their choice.

McREL & AASL/AECT Standards same as Lesson 1—Part 1

The next step is to get the family involved. Inform and involve parents/guardians as early as possible. The family serves an important role and their support is greatly needed. Robert Sylwester tells us "truly engaged students will actually do much of their exploring and learning during non-school time, thus expanding the curriculum." (Sylwester, 2000: 24)

First Session

- The first step is for each student to take home the "I-Search Topic Homework" assignment sheet. (See Figure 3-10.) After the final skim-and-scan library trip, give students the homework.

I-Search Topic Homework

1. **Take your first three topic choices home to share with your family.**

2. **Discuss your family's ideas and suggestions.**

3. **Make a decision based on your interests and whether there is enough information available to write a good research paper and product.**

4. **Return this homework to your teacher to be added to your I-Search Journal.**

I-Search Topic _____

Student _____

Parent _____

Date _____

Figure 3-10. I-Search Topic Homework

- This involves students taking their top three choices home and sharing them with their family. The students need to share what was found in the library and discuss the suggestions and ideas with family members.

- Based on the discussion, information, availability of materials, and interest, students are asked to make their decision. They complete the assignment sheet, sign it and have their parent/guardian sign it.

Second Session

- Check the homework sheets upon their return to make sure everyone is on the right track with his/her topic selection. Set up conferences for those students who are still having trouble.

- Spend a lot of time helping students choose their topic. This should help them choose a topic that is meaningful and will carry them through the research process.

- The last step of this process is to have the students write a rough draft of a paper entitled "Why I chose …." Have them write about the reasons for choosing their topic. They should not worry about spelling or punctuation at this time.

- Share and discuss the writing in small groups. Place the draft in I-Search Journal after teacher review.

Lesson 2: Develop the Questions— Parts 1 and 2	Two to three 30–45- minute sessions	Teacher/Team/LMS

Choosing a topic and developing questions are basic components of the I-Search process. Teachers and the LMS need to devote time to help students develop well-thought-out topics and questions so that the research will be more meaningful and successful. Dedicating the time and effort to this preliminary work will prove to be more favorable than one day announcing to the students that they need to choose a topic from a jar and then go to the library to do research. When research is done that way, students have insufficient direction and valuable library and research time is wasted. Students may also miss the opportunity to connect to a subject, to ask good questions, and to be involved in a community of enthusiastic learners. Take the time to get started in a comprehensive and meaningful way. It is worth it!

Lesson 2: Part 1— Develop Big and Little Questions	One 30–45-minute session	LMS responsible Teacher/Team support

Materials Needed

- Big and Little Questions T-Chart on poster, transparency, or chart paper
- Colored markers or transparency pens

Lesson Objective

Students will have the opportunity to determine the difference between Big and Little questions.

McREL Standards/Benchmarks—Language Arts—4th Ed.

- Standard 4: Gathers and uses information for research purposes.

    1. Uses a variety of strategies to plan research.

- Standard 7: Uses reading skills and strategies to understand a variety of informational texts.

    1. Uses prior knowledge and experience to understand and respond to new information.

AASL/AECT Information Literacy Standards

- Standard 4: The student who is an independent learner is information literate and pursues information related to personal interests.

Anticipatory Set

- Discuss with students the need to ask higher-level questions when doing research.

Point out the difference between Big and Little questions. Little questions often begin with *what, where, who,* and *when* while Big questions begin typically with *why* or *how.*

Guided Practice

- Practice identifying Big and Little questions by asking one of the students to be interviewed while pretending to be a character from a book or video used in the introductory activities. Use a T-Chart to record the questions under Big or Little. (See Figure 3-11.)

Big Questions	Little Questions

Figure 3-11. Research Activity

- Have students ask the volunteer questions about the book or video. After the questions are answered, have students decide whether it was a big or little question depending on how it was asked and answered. Little questions have little, short answers. Big questions have big answers that are elaborated.
- Record the questions in the proper column on the T-Chart.

Group Discussion (Ask students)

- How does someone answer a Big question?
- How does someone answer a Little question?
- When do you learn the most about a person or situation?
- Which kinds of questions will give you the most information?

Closure/Input/Reflection

- Ask students to think about the difference between Big and Little questions. Think about examples of each.
- Have students share their thoughts with their neighbor.
- Discuss the differences as a class. Call on several students to share their thoughts.

(From *The Mindful School: How to Teach for Metacognitive Reflection,* by Robin Fogarty. © 1994 by IRI/Skylight Training and Publishing. Reprinted by permission of LessonLab, a Pearson Education Company, www.lessonlab.com.)

Lesson 2: Part 2— Develop Research Questions	One 45–60-minute session	Teacher/Team LMS support

Materials Needed

- Question Chart (Figure 3-12) on transparency, poster, or chart
- Different colored transparency pens
- Student I-Search Journals
- Overhead projector

Lesson Objective

Students will utilize their skills developing higher- and lower-level questions when creating their own I-Search questions.

McREL Standards/Benchmarks same as Lesson 2—Part 1

Anticipatory Set and Introduction

- Explain to students that good researchers research with a purpose. They search for the answers to questions they have. Tell students that they are becoming good researchers and that today they will create their questions for their own research.
- Review the difference between Big and Little questions.

Modeling

- Show a blank Question Chart (see Figure 3-12) on the overhead.
- Brainstorm in think-aloud fashion, "What do I know" about the topic. List only the keywords. (For example, what do I know about Southern quilts? See Figure 3–13)
- Next, brainstorm in the same fashion, "What do I want to find out?" Again, list only the key words. (See second column Figure 3–13 and model listing items on your chart.)

Independent Practice

- Ask students to turn to the Question Chart on page one of their "I-Search Journal."
- Have students list what they know about their topic in the first column, "What do I know?"
- Have students then list the things they want to find out about their topic in column two. Remind them to refer to the time they skimmed and scanned and discovered things they wanted to learn more about.
- Have students share their lists with their partners and make needed corrections.
- Monitor the students.

What do I know?	What do I want to find out?	What are my research questions?

"Pre-Notetaking Sheet" source: Joyce, Marilyn L. and Julie I. Tallman. 1997. *Making the Writing and Research Connection with the I-Search Process: A How-to-Do-It Manual for Teachers and School Librarians.* Reprinted with permission from the Publisher. Copyright © 1997 by Neal-Schuman Publishers, Inc.

Figure 3-12. Question Chart

What do I know?	What do I want to find out?	What are my research questions?
Old clothes Pretty cloth Different designs Cut out shapes Cover beds	*Slave Quilts* *Maps* Decorations *Patterns* *Designs* Keepsake	How did the slaves in the South use quilts as maps? Why? What are some famous Southern quilt patterns and designs? How do people in the South use quilts? Why? Concept question: How did quilts describe the environment, lifestyles, beliefs, and struggles of the slaves in the South before the Civil War? What is other interesting information about quilts?

"Pre-Notetaking Sheet" source: Joyce, Marilyn L. and Julie I. Tallman. 1997. *Making the Writing and Research Connection with the I-Search Process*. New York: Neal-Schuman. Reprinted with permission from the publisher. Copyright © 1997 by Neal-Schuman Publishers, Inc.

Figure 3-13. Completed Question Chart

Modeling with Independent Practice

- The next activity requires students to group items that go together. The purpose of this activity is to put similar questions together so that research questions will not be repeated.

1. Show students your Question Chart.
2. Read over the list and put a star by those things that are of most interest.
3. Have students repeat the above process.
4. Read over the list and draw an oval around those things that go together.
5. Monitor students as they repeat the above process.
6. Put a rectangle around those things that go together.
7. Monitor students as they repeat the process.
8. Put a starburst around additional things that go together.
9. Monitor students as they repeat the process if needed.

(Refer to Figure 3-13 for an example of a completed Question Chart.)

Modeling with Guided Practice

- At the top of the Question Sheet, list *Who, What, Where, When, Why,* and *How.*

These words lend themselves to higher-level questions. Students then repeat the above process on their Question Chart.

- Take the first item from the first column; in the second column, model turning it into a formal research question. Also, model how to combine items that go together from the first column. Model developing two research questions and then have the students try one. (Again, refer to Figure 3-13 as an example.)
- Explain to students that developing higher-level questions will make their research better. Many times they only need to add the words "Why" or "How" to make it a higher-level question. Sometimes, however, it is

important to create a little question because higher-level questions may build on them.

• As students finish, have them share. Check to see if everyone is on the right track and understands the process. Model developing the rest of the questions and then have them do the same. Slow the process down if they are struggling.

• Research questions should include questions dealing with the unit concept. For example: How did quilts describe the environment, lifestyles, beliefs, and struggles of the slaves in the South before the Civil War? (See Figures 3-6 and 3-13.)

Closure/Input/Reflection

Have students share their questions with one another.

• Call on several students to share their questions. Ask the class if the questions are Big or Little.

• Collect the I-Search Journals to review participation, understanding of the process, and student-generated questions. Using the Standards-Based Grade Sheet in Chapter 7, note those who completed the requirement and those who have not.

• Set up conferences with those who are struggling. If a similar problem emerges in many of the students' Question Charts, develop a quick mini-lesson to clear up the problem.

(Lesson taken from *I-Search, You Search, We All Learn to Research* by Duncan and Lockhart, © 2000, Neal-Schuman Publishers, Inc.)

Lesson 3: Develop I-Search Action Plan	One 30–45-minute session	Teacher/Team LMS support

Materials Needed

• I-Search Action (Figure 3-14) and I-Search Action Plan (Figure 3-15)

• Wall calendar

• Student I-Search Journals

• Transparency of a Note Sheet (Figure 5-1)

I-SEARCH ACTION

QUESTION   When I develop questions

EXPLORE   When I find information

CREATE   When I use the information I find

PRESENT   When I share my information and ideas

JUDGE   When I decide if I did my best

©Roger von Oech. 1986. From *A Kick in the Seat of the Pants*. For more information go to http://creativethink.com.

Figure 3-14. I-Search Action

I-SEARCH ACTION PLAN

5. How will I know I did a good job?

1. What do I want to know?

4. How will I show what I learned?

2. Where can I find the information?

3. How will I understand and record the information?

Figure 3-15. I-Search Action Plan

- Product, I-Search paper, and presentation rubrics mounted on posters around room and additional copies for students
- Copies of homework and contract for each student (Figure 3-16)

Lesson Objective

Students will develop an I-Search Action Plan and continue to compile a personal I-Search Journal.

McREL Standards/Benchmark—Language Arts, 4th ed.

- Standard 4: Gathers and uses information for research purposes.
    1. Uses a variety of strategies to plan research (develops a course of action; determines necessary information).

AASL/AECT Information Literacy Standards

- Standard 4: The student who is an independent learner is information literate and pursues information related to personal interests.

Anticipatory Set

- Explain to students that plans need to be made and goals set in order to make learning successful. They will need to decide what they need to know, where to find the answers, how they will record what they find, and what will be the results of their findings (new recipe, making the trip, toy, or craft). Finally, how will they know that they did a good job (the cookies were good, the trip was successful, the toy or craft worked)?
- Refer students to their I-Search questions. They developed questions and now they need to finish their plan so that they will know where they are going and how they will get there. The five I-Search Action words for planning are *question, explore, create, present, judge.*

I-Search Product Homework

1. Take your list of product choices and the rubrics home to share with your family.

2. Discuss the suggestions with them.

3. Review the rubric for your product.

4. Make a decision about the product you want to make.

5. Sign the attached product contract.

6. Return the product contract to your teacher.

Product Contract

My product is going to be a _____ . My presentation and product will include all the answers to my questions and any additional information I feel is important. I will follow the specific guidelines found on the rubric for my product.

I will have my product ready at the beginning of class on _____ .

Student _____

Parent _____

Teacher _____

Date _____

Please return this sheet. You may keep the product rubric at home in order to check the requirements while working on your product. Thank you and have fun!

Figure 3-16. Product Homework and Contract

Question! Explore! Create! Present! Judge!

Explain each of these terms and their meaning to your students. A skit or other activity might add interest and help them remember what they mean. (See Figure 3-14.)

- Also review the steps of the I-Search Action Plan. Using a transparency, computer, poster, or chart, illustrate the connection between the five action words and the I-Search Action Plan. (See Figure 3-15.)

- Clarify that this is a starting point and that students will adjust and change the plan as needed. For example, sometimes they may have additional questions they would like to ask. They may also discover new places to find information that they will need to add. Lastly, explain that sometimes a student may initially choose a product to show his or her learning but realize during the research that another product would show his or her learning better. For example, a student may initially choose to show learning using a poster but discover that a PowerPoint presentation or diorama would illustrate the information better. Refer to the I-Search Journal and Chapter 6 for a list of possible products.

Guided Practice

- Refer students to the developed questions from their completed question chart. Students should list their questions on the "What do I want to know?" section of the I-Search Action Plan (see Figure 3-17) located in their I-Search Journals.

- Brainstorm with the class about resources that will help them find the answers to their questions. Students need to record these resources on the "Where can I find the information?" section of the plan. (See Figure 3-18.) This is just preliminary information to get students started. It will grow and develop as students learn more about the library and Internet sites.

- Discuss what will be used to record the information they find and how they will give credit to their sources. Show them an example of a Note Sheet. Describe how it is used and have them check "note sheet" in the "How will I understand and record the information I find?" section of the I-Search Action Plan. Briefly discuss the search log, resource finder, main idea graphic, summary board, summary of the search, and the I-Search paper. (See Figure 3-19.)

What Do I Want to Know?

1. _____

2. _____

3. _____

4. _____

5. _____

Figure 3-17. What Do I Want to Know?

Where Can I Find the Information?

1. _____

2. _____

3. _____

4. _____

5. _____

Figure 3-18. Where Can I Find the Information?

How Will I Understand and Record the Information I Find?

- _____Note Sheets

- _____Search Log

- _____Resource Finder

- _____Main Idea Graphic

- _____Summary Board

- _____Summary of the Search

Figure 3-19. How Will I Understand and Record the Information I Find?

How Will I Show What I Learned?

- Date due: _____ I-Search Paper _____

- Date due: _____ Product _____

- Date due: _____ Presentation _____

- Date due: _____ I-Search Journal Portfolio _____

Figure 3-20. How Will I Show What I Learned?

- Discuss what will be done with the information and how students will show what they have learned. Present the product options and show examples to the students. Let them know that they need to make a preliminary decision today about their product. They will be able to change their choice of products right before they use their research to do the project. Have students fill in paper, product choice, and due dates in the "How will I show what I learned?" section of the I-Search Plan. (See Figure 3-20.)

- Discuss the Product Contract. The Product Contract and rubric are sent home early in the I-Search Unit process in order to make the family aware of the project and when it is due. The contract is signed and returned to the teacher. The contract will be sent home again at the end of the research. (See Figure 3-16.)

- Discuss how the students will know they did a good job. Review the checklist on the I-Search Action Plan in the "How will I know I did a good job?" section and the rubrics that will be used to assess the projects. (See Figure 3-21.)

- Putting due dates on a wall calendar creates another visual reminder.

- Congratulate your students for making a plan for their research. Encourage them to refer often to their I-Search Action Plan for guidance and to adjust their information. They have begun with the end in mind.

Closure/Input/Reflection

- Pulling it Together Questions—This activity is valuable when you want your students to begin learning a process that they can use elsewhere and in many different areas of their learning. Have students individually reflect and work through the following questions in their I-Search Journal:

  - What did we accomplish by using the I-Search Action Plan?

  - Why did we do what we did?

  - How might we be able to use what we did at another time?

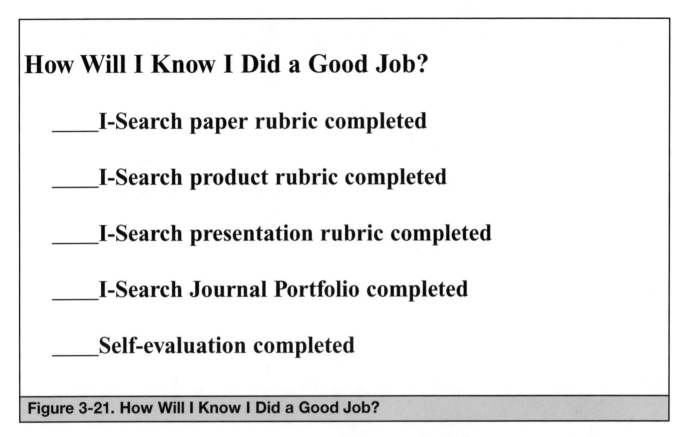

How Will I Know I Did a Good Job?

_____I-Search paper rubric completed

_____I-Search product rubric completed

_____I-Search presentation rubric completed

_____I-Search Journal Portfolio completed

_____Self-evaluation completed

Figure 3-21. How Will I Know I Did a Good Job?

Debrief and discuss in small groups or as a whole class.

- Collect the I-Search Journals to review students' I-Search Action Planners for understanding and completeness. You can also circulate during the activity to check for mastery.

- Mixed abilities are a reality in most classrooms. The I-Search Unit process lends itself to differentiation for the needs of individual learners. Students who are ready may develop more questions and be able to research independently. Others may show their learning at a higher level through product choice, writing, and presentation. You will also be able to pull small groups of learners together to reinforce strategies and reteach when necessary. The next three chapters include lessons that break down the research skills into specific reading, writing, speaking, and listening activities. You will be able to introduce skills and evaluate student readiness while adjusting to the needs of each learner.

4 WHERE CAN WE FIND THE INFORMATION?

INTRODUCTION

Guiding students through the seemingly endless supply of information is daunting! "Google alone is probed more than 138,000 times a minute in 90 languages. In the course of a day that's over 200 million searches of 6 billion Web pages, images and discussion group postings." (Levy, 2004: 50) Kathy Schrock writes:

> The acquisition of digital literacy skills is dependent upon the student's ability to find information, determine its usefulness and accuracy, and utilize it effectively … therefore, the ability to critically evaluate information is an invaluable skill in this information age. (Schrock, 2002: 1)

Students can access and evaluate online information if they have the reading skills to do so. "Doing research is exciting for children, but not if they have difficulty reading their references. If we want students to use nonfiction when they research, we have to teach them how to read nonfiction." (Laase and Clemmons, 1998: 11)

Reading strategies integrated into the I-Search process will improve students' comprehension, especially with informational text including the Internet. Nell K. Duke writes that to improve students' comprehension of informational texts as early as K–3 teachers should:

- Increase students' access to informational text.
- Increase the time students spend working with informational text in instructional activities.
- Explicitly teach comprehension strategies.
- Create opportunities for students to use informational text for authentic purposes. (Duke, 2004: 40)

These activities will help students learn to "navigate and comprehend nonfiction texts throughout the year. This will help them succeed on the critical (standardized) tests." (Boynton and Blevins, 2004: 9)

Reading strategies based on language arts standards/benchmarks and reading and writing objectives that are often found on standardized tests are located throughout the I-Search Unit process. They include:

- Developing questions
- Fostering careful reader strategies
- Offering context clues and vocabulary development
- Using guide words
- Taking notes/citing sources
- Learning to make predictions
- Developing meaning/reciprocal teaching
- Differentiating fact and opinion
- Summarizing, sequencing information, and drawing conclusions
- Determining main idea
- Inferring

Teachers and the LMS working collaboratively can provide instruction that helps students make an emotional connection to this learning, use the latest technology to solve their information problems, and have opportunities to increase their reading and writing skills. These are the critical connections between the standards, assessment, and evidence-based practice that help improve student achievement.

Lesson 4: Establish Careful Reader Strategies	One 30–45-minute session	Teacher/Team or LMS

Materials Needed

- High interest book on the unit topic
- What a Careful Reader Does! chart/poster (Figure 4-1)
- Transparency of key pages of book where students will find answers to your prepared questions (be sure and follow copyright law and get permission if needed) or several copies of the book
- Sticky notes
- I-Search Journal for each student

Lesson Objective

Students will have the opportunity to acquire new vocabulary from context and to learn to go back into the text for answers in preparation for taking notes during the research process.

McREL Standards/Benchmarks—Language Arts, 4th ed.

- Standard 5: Uses the general skills and strategies of the reading process.
    1. Previews text.
    2. Establishes a purpose for reading.
    7. Understands level-appropriate reading vocabulary.
    8. Monitors own reading strategies and makes modifications as needed.

AASL/AECT Information Literacy Standards

- Standard 2: The student who is information literate evaluates information critically and competently.

Anticipatory Set

- Choose a high-interest book (fiction or nonfiction) on the unit topic and read it to the class. For example, *Abuela* by Arthur Dorrus is a good choice for a unit on National Heritage.
- Go through all the steps that a careful reader follows before, during, and after reading. These steps can be posted in the classroom so that students can refer to them at all times. (See Figure 4-1.)

What a Careful Reader Does

Before reading, a careful reader asks:

- **Why am I reading this story or article?**

- **What does this seem to be about?**
    Is it about something or someone I already know?
    Is it about something new I am learning?
    Is it about something I want to learn?

- **What kind of reading will I do?**
    Will I read about characters in a story?
    Will I read about how to do something?
    Will I read to learn interesting facts?

During reading, a careful reader asks:

- **Do I understand what I'm reading?**
    Can I figure out any words I don't know?
    Do I need to slow down?
    Do I need to look for clues?
    Do I need to read some parts again?

- **How can I connect with what I'm reading?**
    Is it something I already know?
    Is it something new I am learning?
    Is it something I want to know more about?

After reading, a careful reader asks:

- **What do I remember about what I read?**
    Can I use my own words to tell others about it?
    Can I name the most important ideas in it?
    Can I think of other ways to show that I understand it?

- **What do I think about what I read?**
    Did it add to something I already knew?
    Did it tell me something new?
    Did it make me want to learn more?

Source: Texas Education Agency. 2003. *Grade 3: TAKS Study Guide*. Austin: TX. Copyright © 2003. Texas Education Agency.

Figure 4-1. What a Careful Reader Does

Guided Practice

- When finished reading the book, ask questions and encourage students to go back into the story to find the answers. Model answering questions from the text.

Sequencing:

1. What happened first in the story?
2. What was the last event after _____?

Setting:

1. Where does the story take place?

Cause and Effect:

1. _____ did _____ because _____ .

Compare and Contrast:

1. What did the characters have in common?
2. Both characters liked/disliked _____ .
3. How were the characters different?

Individual Practice

Possible instructional strategies to help students learn to go back into the text and find answers to their questions include:

- Using transparencies of key pages and excerpts from the book that was read aloud. Have students work individually or with a partner to study the transparency and find the answers to the questions. They can then go the overhead projector and underline the answers.
- Having several copies of the book that was read aloud and having students work together in groups to answer questions by placing sticky notes where they find the answers.

Closure/Input/Reflection:

Think/Pair/Share:

- Teacher or LMS poses question to students: Based on this activity, what have you learned that you can continue to use?
- Students think about the question and construct a response. They share their ideas with a neighbor.
- Teacher/LMS records students' ideas
- Emphasize the importance of going back into the text to find answers to questions. This is an important reading and research skill.

(Adapted from Silver, Strong, and Perini, *Tools for Promoting Active In-Depth Learning, 2nd ed.* Woodbridge, NJ: Thoughtful Education Press. © 2001 by Thoughtful Education Press L.L.C. Reprinted with permission, *www.thoughtful.com*.)

Lesson 5: Incorporate Context Clues and Vocabulary Development	One to two 30–45-minute sessions	Teacher/Team or LMS

Materials Needed

- Transparency, chart or poster of context clues (Figure 4-2)
- Book used in Lesson Four
- Transparency, chart, or poster of Wonderful Words chart (Figure 4-3)
- Copies of Wonderful Words chart for students (Figure 4-3)
- Textbook unit of study or reference books such as encyclopedias
- I-Search Journals for each student

Objective

Students will have opportunities to build and visualize vocabulary, develop dictionary skills, and participate in group work while learning to use context clues to discover the meanings of words they may encounter as they read and research.

McREL Standards/Benchmarks—Language Arts, 4th ed.

- Standard 4: Gathers and uses information for research purposes.

    4. Uses dictionaries to gather information for research topics.

AASL/AECT Information Literacy Standards

- Standard 1: The student who is information literate accesses information efficiently and effectively.

Anticipatory Set

- While researching, students may come across many words that are unfamiliar to them. They will need to be able to learn what these words mean so that they can understand what they are reading in order to answer their questions.

- They can use context clues to discover the meanings of words. Context clues are the "clues" to learning the meaning of words in relation to other words. These clues are actually in what they read and are often near the word they are trying to understand.

- Review different types of context clues on an overhead, chart, or poster. (See Figure 4-2.)

- Model the skill by using the book used in Lesson Four to review the different ways to learn words.

- Find a word that may be unfamiliar to the students and record it on a transparency, chart, or poster of the Wonderful Words chart. (See Figure 4-3.)

- Think aloud. Read the sentences around the word and find the context clue that helps the students understand the word.

- Record what students think the word means or guess the meaning and write it on the transparency.

- Model using the dictionary to look up the actual meaning of the word. Use guide words and other dictionary skills to find the word. Use transparencies or other visuals to illustrate the guide word.

- Draw a picture, chart, or graph to show the meaning of the word on the Figure 4-3 transparency.

CONTEXT CLUES

Synonym—A word that means the same or almost the same thing as another word (big and large).

*It takes a long time to **construct** a bridge. Workers took several years to **build** the Golden Gate Bridge.*

Antonym—A word that means the opposite of another word (hot and cold).

*The lion looked **tame** but it was **wild**.*

Explanations, Definitions, and Descriptions—A group of words that define, explain, or describe the meaning of another word.

*Todd was in the **choir** at his old school. He hopes his new school will also have a **group that sings songs together**.*

Example—An example is an item that belongs in a group because it is like other things in the group.

*Tran wants to be an **author** when he grows up. He wants to write like his favorite author, **Dr. Seuss**.*

Source: Texas Education Agency. 2003. *Grade 3: TAKS Study Guide*. Austin: TX. Copyright © 2003. Texas Education Agency.

Figure 4-2. Context Clues

Wonderful Words

WORD	GUESS THE MEANING	DICTIONARY DEFINITION	PICTURE OF DEFINITION

Figure 4-3. Wonderful Words

Guided Practice

- Next, lead students through a guided practice of the above activity on their own chart:

    1. Choose the word and have everyone record it in the first column.

    2. Find the word in the literature and read around it. Have students guess what the word means and explain why.

    3. Have everyone record his or her guesses.

    4. Pass out the dictionaries and lead everyone through the process of locating the word.

    5. Record the actual definition.

    6. Brainstorm with students about what they could draw to show the meaning. Have them complete the last section.

Independent Practice

- Use science or social studies textbooks or other reference books such as encyclopedias and find a word for which students can discover the meaning. Have them repeat the above process. Check for understanding.

- Students have begun their Wonderful Words chart. This activity will continue throughout the unit. It can be used as closure activities and as activity anchors. You may require a certain number of words to be recorded on the chart during the unit.

- Students should store their charts with their I-Search Journals.

Closure/Input/Reflection

- Journal Reflection—Instruct students to think about what they did well. Have them write and finish this prompt: I feel _____ because I _____.

- Feeling words that can be reviewed and posted in the classroom are: happy, satisfied, joyous, ecstatic, enthusiastic, cheerful, excited, exhilarated, jolly, thrilled, proud.

Lesson 6: Design Keyword Searches	One 30–45-minute session	LMS with Teacher/Team Support

Materials Needed

- I-Search Action Plan/Student I-Search Journal for each student
- LMC resources such as electronic or print general/special encyclopedia indices, reference sources such as dictionaries, almanacs, atlases, and online catalogs and the indices of information books related to the unit
- Library workstations

Lesson Objective

Students will determine key words in their I-Search questions and locate those words in reference sources.

McREL Standards/Benchmarks—Language Arts, 4th Ed.

- Standard 4: Gathers and uses information for research purposes.
  5. Uses keywords, guide words, alphabetical and numerical order, indices, cross-references, and letter on volumes to find information for research topics.

AASL/AECT Information Literacy Standards

- Standard 2: The student who is information literate evaluates information critically and competently.

Anticipatory Set

- Begin the lesson by displaying a sample question based on a unit concept on a poster, chart, or transparency.
- Brainstorm with students about possible keywords in the question. Underline the words in each question.
- Discuss the fact that all the words will not lead to information being sought. Some words will be dropped and others added during the search.

Guided Practice

- Model finding the keywords on a projected transparency of an index from a textbook or reference book.
- Circle each keyword as the class finds it.

Individual and Group Practice

- Students find the keywords in their I-Search questions.
- Have students work in small groups to find keywords in reference materials at prearranged workstations in the LMC.
- The LMS will describe the materials at the workstations.
- Materials at the workstations may include information books related to the unit, indices of reference books, online encyclopedias, almanacs/atlases/dictionaries on CD-ROM, and the online catalog.
- Students will record on their Keyword Pathfinder the reference sources where they find keywords. (See Figure 4-4.)
- The teacher and LMS should work with small groups of students, reteaching the concept and discussing the process as needed.

Closure/Input/Reflection

- Bring the class together and discuss which resources had the most keywords.
- Remind students to keep their keyword search in their I-Search Journals to use when they do further research.

Lesson 7: Develop Meaning with Reciprocal Teaching	One 45–60-minute session	Teacher/Team or LMS

"Incorporating information text in the curriculum in the early years of school has the potential to increase student motivation, build important comprehension skills, and lay the groundwork for students to grow into confident, purposeful readers." (Duke, 2004: 43) One of the most effective ways to build comprehension skills is to use the reciprocal

Keyword	Source
	Title_____ Author/Publisher_____ Call Number/Web site_____
	Title_____ Author/Publisher_____ Call Number/Web site_____
	Title_____ Author/Publisher_____ Call Number/Web site_____
	Title_____ Author/Publisher_____ Call Number/Web site_____
	Title_____ Author/Publisher_____ Call Number/Web site_____

Figure 4-4. Keyword Pathfinder

teaching strategy. It allows the teaching of "multiple strategies simultaneously." (Duke, 2004: 42)

Rogers, Ludington, and Graham tell us that the purpose of reciprocal teaching is to "facilitate students gaining an understanding from their reading." They go on to say that in many cases, students know how to read, but they don't possess effective strategies for developing meaning from what they are reading. This is a process that many successful readers either developed on their own or picked up along the way from their teachers. (1998: 194)

Students need practice with the reciprocal teaching process before they can be expected to implement it on their own.

Materials Needed

- Article from textbook, reference book, or online source.
- Reciprocal Teaching chart. (See Figure 4-5.)
- Blank paper or letter template on computers for each student.
- I-Search Student Journals. (See Figure 4-5.)

Lesson Objective

Students will be introduced to reading strategies that will help them develop meaning from what they are reading and researching.

McREL Standards/Benchmarks—Language Arts, 4th ed.

- Standard 1: Uses the general skills and strategies of the writing process.

    12. Writes personal letters.

- Standard 5: Uses the general skills and strategies of the reading process.

    1. Previews text.

    2. Establishes a purpose for reading.

    3. Makes, confirms, and revises simple predictions about text.

    8. Monitors own reading strategies and makes modifications as needed.

    9. Adjusts speed of reading to suit purpose and difficulty of the material.

AASL/AECT Information Literacy Standards

Standard 1: The student who is information literate accesses information efficiently and effectively.

Standard 3: The student who is information literate uses information accurately and creatively.

Introduction

- Explain to students that in order to find the answers to their questions they need to put together many of the reading strategies such as developing questions, summarizing information, making predictions, and clarifying what they have learned.

- All these strategies combined are called Reciprocal Teaching. It is used when we read fiction or nonfiction text. It helps us understand what we are reading.

- The steps of Reciprocal Teaching are summarizing, questioning, clarifying, and predicting. (See Figure 4-5.)

Guided Practice

- Have students form reading groups of five.

- Model the following activity on the overhead. The teacher should act as the "summarizer."

- The students should each read a paragraph from a textbook information, reference book, or online article dealing with the unit concept.

- Have one student (the summarizer) in each group summarize what was read. Explain to students that a good summary includes information from the beginning, middle, and end of the paragraph. Other members of the group may add to the summary in an orderly, predetermined manner.

- The student summarizer asks information-gathering questions of his or her group. The purpose of this step is to bring out specific information from the short passage that supports the summary.

RECIPROCAL TEACHING

Summarizing

Questioning

Clarifying

Predicting

Figure 4-5. Reciprocal Teaching

- The summarizers then ask questions of their groups to help ensure clarity/understanding. Other members of the group may also ask questions such as: "I didn't quite understand the part about _____. Can someone explain what was meant?

- The summarizer then asks the members of his or her group to predict what will be in the next section to be read. The groups should record the predictions on chart paper.

- Each group selects a new summarizer and the process continues.
- This activity can be repeated with any text. Students should be encouraged to consciously engage in the four parts of Reciprocal Teaching when they are reading, researching, and studying on their own.

Closure and Research Connection

- Review how the information from the activities relates to the unit. Discuss the connections and new learning.
- Note to a Friend—Review of the Reciprocal Teaching process
  1. Tell students to pretend a friend has been absent from class and they are going to describe the learning that their friend missed in the form of a friendly letter.
  2. Describe to the students the major parts of a friendly letter or have them work on computers where letter templates have been set up on the computers.
  3. Review with students the major points of the Reciprocal Teaching process.
  4. Have students create their own ideas regarding effective ways to communicate with text, diagrams, and/or pictures.
  5. Finally, have the students review the rough drafts of their letters to check for clarity and errors.
  6. The final copies of their letters should go into their I-Search Journals.

"Reciprocal Teaching" and "Note From a Friend" from *Motivation and Learning*, by Spence Rogers, Jim Ludington and Shari Graham © Peak Learning Systems, Inc. Printed with permission from Peak Learning Systems, Inc. Evergreen, Colorado, (303) 679-9780, *www.peaklearn .com*.

Ongoing Assessment

Review and assess "Letter to a Friend" to check for understanding.

Lesson 8: Interview Experts	One 30–45-minute session	Teacher/Team or LMS

Materials Needed

- Overhead projector
- Transparency of Interview Etiquette (Figure 4-6)
- Blank transparencies and transparency pens
- Transparency of Interview Form (Figure 4-7)
- Copy of Interview Etiquette and Interview Form for each student
- Blank chart and markers
- Books about a person's story
- Parent permission letter
- Expert on unit topic

Lesson Objective

Students will learn how to conduct an interview and summarize information learned in the interview.

McREL Standards/Benchmarks—Language Arts, 4th ed.

- Standard 8: Uses listening and speaking strategies for different purposes.
  2. Asks questions in class.
  3. Responds to questions and comments.
  4. Listens to classmates and adults.

AASL/AECT Information Literacy Standards

- Standard 9: The student who contributes positively to the learning community and to society is information literate and participates effectively in groups to pursue and generate information.

Anticipatory Set/Attention Getter

- Review the work done for Step Two of the I-Search Plan. Remind students that people and experts were mentioned as sources of information as well as print and online sources. They should understand that "conducting oral interviews is a worthwhile way for student researchers to gain access to information." (Moore, Moore, Cunningham, and Cunningham, 1998: 288)

- Role-play an interview in order to help students prepare to conduct their own interviews. Read a story about someone in history and then have one of the students pretend to be that person and let the class interview him or her. Remind students to ask Big questions as well as Little questions. *The Story of Ruby Bridges* by Robert Coles is a good book to continue the national heritage emphasis.

Guided Practice

- Reflect on the role-played interview. Ask students what makes a good interview. What did they observe that was effective? What could have been done better?

- Review interview etiquette with the class. See Figure 4-6.

- Tell the students about the expert who will visit the class. Use the interview form to formulate questions to ask the expert. Record the questions on the transparency and have students copy them on their interview forms. They should keep the forms in their I-Search Journal. (See Figure 4-7.)

- Invite an expert to your class for the class interview. Remind students not to write every word but to summarize the expert's answers. There is more on note-taking in Chapter 5.

Individual Practice

- Have students write summary paragraphs about the expert based on the notes they took during the class interview.

- An extension and differentiation activity would encourage students to find experts and interview them outside of school. Students would need parent permission and supervision. Send a note home updating parents/guardians on the activities and learning being done. Elicit their help in setting up interviews.

Interview Etiquette

1. Experts and authorities are helpful sources of information when you are doing research. These people are those who know a lot about something. They do not need to hold an official position.

2. Contact the person with a letter, phone call, fax, and/or e-mail before interviewing them. Decide which way is the best approach for your situation.

3. Take careful notes. If a tape recorder is used, be sure to ask permission to use it.

4. Your questions need to be prepared ahead of time. However, ask additional questions if you see a good opportunity.

5. Ask your experts where they go to find more information and answers.

6. Be sure to ask questions that require more than just a "yes" or "no" answer (ask "Big questions").

7. Close the interview with a thank you. Let them know that you appreciate their time. You may also want to send a thank-you note.

Figure 4-6. Interview Etiquette

Closure/Input/Reflection

- Have students share their summary paragraphs in small groups and compare the similarities and differences.
- Students who do independent interviews should be given an opportunity to share them with the class.
- Discuss as a class what makes a good interview. Record students' comments on a chart and post it in the classroom.
- Share with students that they will use the skills they have learned as they continue to research during this unit and throughout school with other research projects.

Interview Form

Name of person interviewed_____

Title of person interviewed_____

Date of interview_____

Person conducting interview_____

    1.   Question:

           Answer:

    2.   Question:

           Answer:

    3.   Question:

           Answer:

    4.   Question:

           Answer:

Put the completed interview form in your I-Search Journal after showing it to your teacher.

Figure 4-7. Interview Form

5 HOW WILL WE UNDERSTAND AND RECORD THE INFORMATION WE FIND?

Chapter 5 Lessons
- Lesson 9: Take Notes and Cite Sources
- Lesson 10: Differentiate Between Fact and Opinion
- Lesson 11: Evaluate Web Site Authenticity
- Lesson 12: Develop Research Workshop Skills
- Lesson 13: Summarize Notes

INTRODUCTION

The third question in the search process is: "How will we understand and record the information we find?" Copying from the encyclopedia or downloading research papers from the Internet is often the practice of researchers no matter their age. The process of gathering, analyzing and synthesizing information in order to make it your own takes time, thought, and ability. These skills do not come naturally, but have to be learned. Today's information society increasingly makes it imperative that students develop these skills. Barbara Jansen tells us:

> Reading for specific information and taking notes may be the most challenging step in the information problem-solving process. Students in grades 3–8 need many developmentally appropriate opportunities to locate and use information before mastering the technique ... More than just extracting needed information, note-taking consists of three steps: identification of keyword and related words in the researchable questions, skimming and scanning, and extracting needed information. (Jansen 2003: 1)

We believe it is never too early to teach students these important skills. Through innovative work by teachers and the LMS, we have found that the task is possible and profitable. Students learn quickly the importance of not copying word for word from their sources. They also learn to summarize the information in their own words and to give credit to their sources.

We utilized the Note Sheet adapted by Corene Madely, a second-grade teacher in Troy Independent School District in Troy, Texas, in *I-Search, You Search, We All Learn to Research*. We continue to find it useful, especially for beginning researchers. One Note Sheet is used for each research question. Students use the "Trash-N-Treasure" method of taking notes to complete the Note Sheet. This method is described in Lesson 9. Students write their question at the top of the Note Sheet and record their notes in the first section. Their source is cited in the box to the right of the notes. Some teachers and LMS list the bibliographic information they deem important in the source box (i.e., title, author, publisher, copyright). There is room for additional notes from another source on the same Note Sheet. Additional Note Sheets may be used for other questions. (See Figure 5-1.)

Lesson 9: Take Notes and Cite Sources	One 45–60-minute session	Teacher/Team or LMS

Materials Needed

- Blank transparency and markers
- Blank sheets of paper for each student
- Picture related to the unit (picture from a book on transparency or poster or computer-generated picture using a multimedia projector)
- Transparency of article that has clearly labeled headings, subheadings, bolded text, graphs, captions, and pictures. The article should address a unit concept in question form
- Copy of separate article for each student. This should also address a unit concept in question form
- Enough Note Sheets for each student to answer his or her question
- Student I-Search Journals (Focus on Figures 5-1 and 5-5)
- A transparency of one of the Note Sheets for demonstration purposes (Figures 5-1 and 5-5)

Note Sheet

Name _____**Topic:**_____

Question:

Notes:	Source:
p.	
Notes:	Source:
p.	

Summary:

Figure 5-1. Note Sheet

Lesson Objective

Students will have the opportunity to access and utilize information resources while learning to take notes and develop specific skills such as comprehension and summarization.

McREL Standards/Benchmarks—Language Arts, 4th ed.

- Standard 1: Uses the general skills and strategies of the writing process.

  1. Prewriting: Uses prewriting strategies to plan written work (e.g., uses graphic organizers, takes notes, brainstorms ideas).

- Standard 4: Gathers and uses information for research purposes.

  7. Uses strategies to gather and record information for research topics (e.g., uses notes and other graphic organizers; paraphrases and summarizes information).

- Standard 7: Uses reading skills and strategies to understand and interpret a variety of informational texts.

  5. Summarizes and paraphrases information in texts.

AASL/AECT Information Literacy Standards

- Standard 1: The student who is information literate accesses information efficiently and effectively.

- Standard 8: The student who contributes positively to the learning community and to society is information literate and practices ethical behavior in regard to information and information technology.

Anticipatory Set

- Explain to students that investigating the details helps us understand what we are reading, observing, and researching. Tell students that we are going to practice looking for details.

- Have each student divide a piece of paper into four squares. Label each square with *who, what, when,* or *where.* Ask students to put *why* on the back of the paper.

- Show a picture related to the unit being studied. It should be detailed enough to answer the questions *who, what, when, where,* and *why.*

- Introduce or review the term "treasure words." Treasure words are the most important words in a sentence or paragraph. They are used when we take notes or jot down ideas in order to save time and space. In her article, "Reading for Information: The Trash-N-Treasure Method of Teaching Note-Taking (Grades 3–12)," Barbara Jansen suggested comparing note-taking to a pirate's treasure map:

    The map itself is like that article or chapter of a book containing information about the topic. The "X" on the map, which marks the exact location of the buried treasure, is the section of the text containing needed information, or an "answer" for specific questions defined in the task. A pirate must dig for the treasure chest, tossing aside dirt, weeds, and rocks (trash). A researcher must dig to find words that help answer the questions (treasure words). He or she must "toss aside" unnecessary sentences, phrases, and words (trash words). Of course, these words are not trash to the original source, only to the researcher because they do not answer the questions defined in the task. These are trash words because they do not answer the research questions. (Jansen, 2003: 4)

- Have students view the picture one more time.

- Ask students to investigate the details and record the "treasure words" that answer each *who, what, when, where,* and *why* question. You may need to model the first two squares or have students work in small groups depending on ability level.

- Have students work in groups to compare results.

- Discuss the information gathered by looking at details.

Guided Practice

- Explain to students that they will be using their observation skills as they search for answers to questions about unit concepts. We will also use the "Trash-N-Treasure" method of taking notes on Note Sheets. This will allow them to get the best and most accurate answers to their questions.

• Before reading the article, describe what the Note Sheet looks like and how it will be used.

• Students have learned the definition and use of treasure words and also that remembering supporting ideas is an important skill. They are now ready to use a Note Sheet.

• Use a transparency of an article from an information/reference book or an online source that answers a question about a unit concept. Explain to the students that they can skim and scan to search for their answers.

  1. Guide students as they look for headings, subheadings, bolded text, graphs, captions, and pictures. Help them locate the appropriate heading.

  2. Find the first sentence and place a slash at the end of it. Read it and ask yourself: "Does this sentence answer the question?"

  3. If the answer is no, tell the students that the sentence is "trash" to them. Go on to the next sentence placing a slash at the end.

  4. If the answer is yes, underline the first phrase and ask if that phrase answers the question. If the answer is no, underline the next phrase and repeat the question.

  5. If the answer is yes, read that phrase word by word, asking which words are needed to answer the question. These are treasure words. Circle those words and write them in the appropriate place on the overhead Note Sheet.

Continue phrase by phrase and word by word until coming to the end of the sentence. Count the words in the sentence and compare to the words used. Discuss how much space was saved and how the treasure words will help them write the summary in their own words. (See Figure 5-2.)

Note Sheet with Notes

Name_____ Topic: Jackie Robinson

Question: Who was Jackie Robinson?

Notes:	Source:
Born Cairo, Georgia, 1919 Youngest five children Grandfather slave Father abandoned family Family moved California Mother washed/ironed clothes make living p.	AOL@School. "Jackie Robinson" www.harcourtschool.com/activity/biographies/robinson/ April 20, 2004
Notes:	Source:
Played basketball, baseball, football, track Joined Army 1942 First African American play baseball Played Brooklyn Dodgers p.	KidsClick. "Jackie Robinson." http://library.thinkquest.org/10320/Robinson.htm April 20, 2004

Summary:

Figure 5-2. Note Sheet with Notes

6. Demonstrate the process again allowing the students to work in groups and practice using copies of another article answering the same question.

7. Provide students the opportunity to independently practice a few times before they begin their own research.

(Note-taking lesson adapted from "Reading for Information: The Trash-N-Treasure Method of Teaching Note-Taking [Grades 3–12]" by Barbara A. Jansen, 2003, *www.big6.com*.)

- The following instructions will explain the importance of giving credit to sources. Explain to students that they are going to take all the notes first and complete the summary boxes later because they may find more information on their question from additional sources.

- Share with them that it is very important to give credit to their sources.

- Relate a story about the difference between borrowing and stealing someone's toy or article of clothing. Explain that stealing someone's words is called plagiarism, but if you borrow their words and give them credit for using them, it's like borrowing a toy or article of clothing.

- Teaching students to cite their sources in the place provided on the note sheet completes the note-taking process at this time. See Figure 5-3 for helpful Web sites on copyright and citing sources.

- Have students fill out the question section for each of their Note Sheets. Students should have a Note Sheet for each of their developed questions. Extra Note Sheets should be made available to the students when they go to the LMC to do research in the event they develop more questions. They should be given the opportunity to research those questions.

- Students may also have more than one source they want to use to answer questions. Staple the Note Sheets together to indicate that they go with the same question.

Citing Sources and Avoiding Plagiarism

Citing Sources:

- "Yahooligans! Teacher's Guide: Citation Sources," provides examples for each grade level K–8 *http://yaholligans.yahoo.com/tg/678.html*

- BibBuilder 1.3 (Free MLA-Style Bibliography Builder) is based on Joseph Gibaldi's *MLA Handbook for Writers of Research Papers*, 4th ed., 1995. *http://jerz.setonhill.edu/writing/academic/bib_builder/index.html*

- NoodleBib is available on a subscription basis to students, teachers, schools and districts. It aids in citing MLA- and APA-style source lists *www.noodletools.com/noodlebib/index.php*

Avoiding Plagiarism:

- *Beyond Technology* by Jamie McKenzie discusses "The New Plagiarism" in Chapter 16. *http://questioning.org*

- Lessons and information on plagiarism are found at: *www.asee.org/prism/december/html/student_plagiarism_in_an_onlin.htm* or *www.cln.org/themes/plagiarism.html*

- Links on Kathy Schrock's Web site include topics such as On Plagiarism; Plagiarism Links; Plagiarized.com; To Copy or Not to Copy: That is the Question. *http://school.discovery.com/schrockguide/reference.html*

Figure 5-3. Citing Sources and Avoiding Plagiarism

• This lesson is an example of taking notes in the traditional manner. Sources for electronic note-taking are listed in Figure 5-4.

Electronic Note Sheets

• *Information Literacy Toolkit: Grades Kindegarten-6* and *Information Literacy Toolkit: Grades 7 and Up* by Jenny Ryan and Steph Capra contain a variety of ideas for taking notes. A CD-ROM that aids in designing the Note Sheets is included with the book.

• Jamie McKenzie and Larry Lewin both have great high-tech ideas for taking notes listed in their books.

• Barbara Jansen's article on the Big 6 Web site, "Ideas About Note Taking and Citing Sources," contains a template for a note-taking form. (*www.big6.com*)

• NoteStar's features include non-Internet sources and notes (e.g., books and magazines articles), with the capability of putting in multiple notes at one time in either APA or MLA format. (*http://notestar.4teachers.org/*)

Figure 5-4. Electronic Note Sheets

Closure/Input/Reflection

• Explain to students that they need to keep track of their research, evaluate how they have done, and make plans for what needs to happen next. This metacognitive reflection provides excellent opportunities for students to increase ownership of their learning. They will be completing a Search Log at the end of each research session. Provide each student with a Search Log (see Figure 5-5) and model the exercise on the overhead:

Date_____

What have I done so far? I learned how to take notes to answer my questions, what plagiarism is, and how to cite sources.

How have I done? I have worked hard and learned a lot.

What do I need to do next? I need to develop more reading and research strategies and begin to answer my questions.

- Store Search Logs in I-Search Journals. (See Figure 5-5.)
- Students can also add words to their Wonderful Words chart by using the resources made available in this lesson.

Ongoing Assessment

- Teachers should collect the I-Search Journals or rotate during the class to review students' work on the note sheets.

Lesson 10: Differentiate Between Fact and Opinion	One 30–45-minute session	Teacher/Team or LMS

Materials Needed

- High-interest book or video that mixes fact and opinion.
- Fact and Opinion graphic organizer on chart or poster. (See Figure 5-6.)
- Fact and Opinion graphic organizer on charts for groups of two/three students.
- Fact and Opinion cards based on the book/video, pre-made by teacher. (See Figure 5-7.)

Lesson Objective

Students will be given the opportunity to develop the skill of differentiating between fact and opinion.

Search Log

Date _____

What have I done so far? _____

How have I done? _____

What do I need to do next? _____

Date: _____

What have I done so far? _____

How have I done? _____

What do I need to do next? _____

Date _____

What have I done so far? _____

How have I done? _____

What do I need to do next? _____

Figure 5-5. Search Log

McREL Standards/Benchmarks—Language Arts, 4th ed.

- Standard 7: Using reading skills and strategies to understand and interpret a variety of informational texts

    1. Uses prior knowledge and experience to understand and respond to new information.

    2. Understands structural patterns or organization in informational texts.

AASL/AECT Information Literacy Standards

- Standard 3: The student who is information literate uses information accurately and creatively.

Anticipatory Set/Explicit Teaching

- Read a high-interest book (such as *A Picture Book of Sojourner Truth* by David Adler) that mixes fact and opinion. Use the Careful Reader Strategies before, during, and after reading the book.

- Have students vote for their favorite part of the book at the conclusion. Point out the many different opinions in the class.

- Explain the difference between fact and opinion.

    1. A fact is something that can be proven true or false.

    2. An opinion cannot be proven true or false. It is what a person thinks or feels.

- Explain to the students that it is important to be able to distinguish between fact and opinion when researching. There is a lot of information in our world that is presented as fact when it is actually someone's opinion. We want our students to develop the ability to gather facts, draw conclusions, and form their own opinions.

Guided Practice

- Give examples of fact and opinion statements from the book. Use a Fact and Opinion graphic organizer either on a chart or on a computer attached to a multimedia projector. See Figure 5-6. Guide students in assigning the facts and opinion cards in the appropriate places. See Figure 5-7 for Fact and Opinion Cards template.

Individual/Group Practice

• Have students create statements of fact and opinion from the book just read or the unit concepts and put them on the Fact and Opinion Cards.

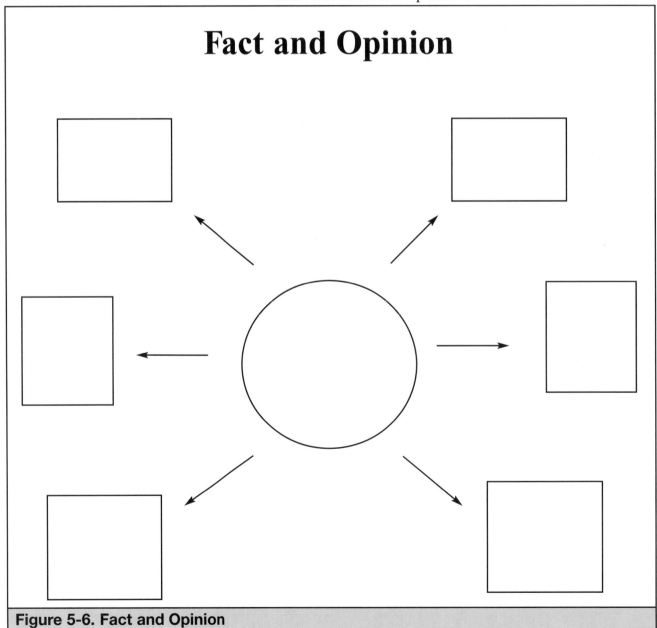

Fact and Opinion

Figure 5-6. Fact and Opinion

Figure 5-7. Fact and Opinion Cards

- Provide poster board, chart paper, or a computer with Kidspiration or similar software and have students work together to create the web, cut out the statements, and glue them in the appropriate squares or, if using the computer, type in the correct information.
- Groups can have different sets of cards and share their graphic organizers with the class when the assignment is completed.
- Discuss how the information learned and reviewed connects to the unit of study.

Closure/Input/Reflection

- Wrap-Up—Have students develop a group response to the following questions:

    1. What were three things we did really well? We know we did well on each of these because _____.

    2. What was one way we could have worked even better together? To do this next time, each of us will _____.

    3. What was the most interesting thing we did? We think so because _____.

    4. What are some of the ways we can use what we learned?

    5. What were some of the things each of us did best?

    6. What is a commitment each of us has made?

- Students can work in their groups and respond in their I-Search Journals to the above statements. They can share this information along with their Fact and Opinion Charts with the class.

(Closure activity from *Motivation and Learning* by Rogers, Ludington, and Graham (c) Peak Learning Systems, Inc. Printed with permission from Peak Learning Systems, Inc. Evergreen, Colorado (303) 679-9780, (*www.peaklearn.com*)

Lesson 11: Evaluate Web Site Authenticity	One 30–45-minute session	LMS or Teacher team

A follow-up lesson to the fact and opinion activity teaches students about the authenticity of Web sites. Larry Lewin, in *Using the Internet to Strengthen Curriculum,* tells us:

> Students are thrilled when they locate Web sites that deal with their chosen topics, but they forget that all sites are not created equally. Some sites are excellent resources with accurate information written by credible people, some sites are decent resources, and some sites are the products of dangerously unstable minds. (Lewin, 2001: 116–117)

Lewin goes on to say, "We want our students to be able to tell the difference between reliable and unreliable Web sites ... and to be critical consumers of information instead of passive recipients." (Lewin, 2001: 118)

Materials Needed

- Computer access for each student
- Internet resources for classroom instruction (Figure 5-8)
- Student I-Search Journals

Lesson Objective

Students will have the opportunity to evaluate Web sites for their authenticity.

McREL Standards/Benchmarks—Language Arts, 4th ed.

- Standard 4: Gathers and uses information for research purposes.
    4. Uses electronic media to gather information (e.g., Internet, databases).
    6. Uses strategies to gather and record information for research topics.

AASL/AECT Information Literacy Standards

- Standard 3: The student who is information literate uses information accurately and creatively.

Anticipatory Set

- Use Kathy Schrock's "Teacher Helpers: Critical Evaluation Information," an extensive site that includes links to critical evaluation surveys, articles by Kathy Schrock, critical evaluation information by others and sites to use for demonstrating critical evaluation to create an introductory activity on Web site evaluation. Information may be found at: *http://school.discovery.com/schrockguide/eval.html.*

Guided Practice

- Share with the students Phil Reinhardt's "Six Questions method for evaluating the quality of information":
  1. **What?** What does the article or information say? Does it answer any question (or part of a question you started with)?
  2. **Where?** Where is the source of this information? Does it have a person's name, organization name, phone number, e-mail address, and site address?
  3. **Who?** Who is the author? Can you get in touch?
  4. **Why?** Why did the author write this information? What is the purpose? Is there a clear point of view? any bias? any important omissions (missing information)?
  5. **When?** When was this information written? Is it current?
  6. **Really?** Is there any way to check the accuracy of the information using other sources? (Lewin, 2001: 118–119)
- Have students do searches for answers to their I-Search questions using the Six Questions method and reliable search engines listed in Figure 5-8.
- Use bogus sites as well, such as *www.bonus.com/bonus/list/beakman.right.html,* to teach the difference between reliable and unreliable sites. Be sure and preview all sites before using them with students. (Lewin, 2001: 118)
- Other helpful sites are found in Figure 5-8.

Independent Practice

- Have students use the Resource Finder (Figure 5-9) to record Web sites that they determine helpful for locating answers to their I-Search questions.

Internet Resources for Classroom Instruction

Books:

- *Beyond Technology: Questioning, Research and the Information Literate School* © 2000 by Jamie McKenzie is full of helpful ideas to guide students through the online research process. (*http://questioning.org*)

- *Using the Internet to Strengthen Curriculum* © 2001 by Larry Lewin walks the reader through the intermediate use of the Web with the "We Search" and through independent use with the "Free Search." (*www.larrylewin.com*)

- *Writing and Research on the Computer* © 2000 by Kathy Schrock, Mary Watkins, and Jan Wahlers includes guidelines for documenting, collecting, searching for, and evaluating information on the Web. (*http://kathyschrock.net/books.htm*)

Online Resources:

- Tutorials for using search engines and subject directories to locate information on the Web (*www.learnwebskills.com/search/main.html*)

- Noodle Tools is a set of interactive tools designed to aid students and professionals with their online research. (*www.noodletools.com/debbie/literacies/information/5locate/adviceengine.html*)

Search Engines for Student Research:

- ALA Great Sites for Kids—*www.ala.org/greatsites*

- Ask Jeeves for Kids—*www.ajkids.com/*

- Awesome Library—*www.awesomelibrary.org/*

- KidsClick!—*sunsite.berkeley.edu/KidsClick!/*

- TekMom's—*www.tekmom.com/search/*

- Yahooligans!—*www.yahooligans.com/*

Figure 5-8. Internet Resources for Classroom Instruction

Resource Finder

Reference Books:	Non-fiction/Information Books:
1.	1.
2	2
3.	3.
4.	4.
Online Reference Sources:	**Online Periodicals:**
1.	1.
2	2
3.	3.
4.	4.
Web Sites:	**Web Sites:**
1.	1.
2	2
3.	3.
4.	4.

Figure 5-9. Resource Finder

Closure/Input/Reflection

- Kindling Activity

    1. Teacher/LMS poses a question—What did you learn how to do today?

    2. Student prompt:

        —One way I will use what I have learned is _____.

        —Students think about the question.

        —Students record ideas in I-Search Journals.

        —Student share their responses in pairs or small groups.

        —Students look for similarities and differences between responses.

        —Students generate new ideas and/or draw conclusions.

(Kindling activity adapted from *Tools for Promoting Active, In-Depth Learning*, 2nd ed. by H. Silver, R. Strong, and M. Perini. (c) 2001 by Thoughtful Education Press, L.L.C. Reprinted with permission.)

Lesson 12: Develop Research Skills Workshop	3–5 Sessions	LMS and Teacher/Team

Armed with the reading and research skills of developing questions, using a research journal, good reader strategies, locating context clues, finding resources, taking notes, making predictions, developing meaning, determining fact and opinion, and evaluating Web sites, students are now ready to put their skills to use and go to the LMC to complete their research. We call this part of the lesson a Research Workshop because it mirrors the structure of the reading/writing workshop. Each research session will begin with a mini-lesson. Students will then work independently and in small groups on their research, reading, and note-taking. The workshop concludes with a brief closure and evaluation of the day using the Search Log.

Advance Preparation

- The LMS and teacher/s decide when classes are scheduled to do research. This needs to be done at the first collaborative planning session for the unit.

• In addition to the list of resources students obtained in their first visit to the library, the LMS and teacher/s will need to provide additional lists of resources and a Resource Finder to help answer student I-Search questions. (See Figure 5-9.)

• The LMS and teacher/s will also need to decide how the research opportunities will be organized. Will the students be in groups that rotate among resource centers or will they work independently? Younger students require group work. Nell K. Duke and V. Susan Bennett-Armistead have excellent ideas for teaching young students how to read, write and use informational text, observation, and interviews that can be found in their book, *Reading & Writing Informational Text in the Primary Grades: Research-Based Practices.*

• An effective method we used and have seen others use is to pair older students with younger students to help them with their research in the library. Whole class research can also be done with the teacher or librarian reading an information/nonfiction book on the unit to the class and as a class taking notes on a poster or chart. Grouping younger students in small groups is also an effective method to facilitate their research.

• Another population that needs to be addressed when setting up a Research Workshop is students with learning difficulties. Susan Winebrenner's *Teaching Kids with Learning Difficulties in the Regular Classroom* has great ideas for student research and "project-based learning." She writes:

> Project-based learning has the potential to "turn on" turned-off students. Teachers have discovered that they can teach the same objectives or outcomes to kids who are working on projects that they would have taught through the regular curriculum. Some teachers worry that struggling students need more teacher control, not less. In fact, the best control comes from letting students immerse themselves in what they are learning. Many behavior problems decrease or disappear. (Winebrenner, 1996: 66)

- Finally, the LMS may need to provide special instruction or mini-lessons at the beginning of each research workshop about how to use various resources. Effective resources for these lessons are *Information Literacy Toolkit, Grades Kindergarten to 6* and *Information Literacy Toolkit, Grades 7 and Up,* written by Jenny Ryan and Steph Capra. In addition, *Developing an Information Literacy Program K–12,* edited by Mary Jo Langhorne, is a good source for innovative ideas.

- Use these learning opportunities to help students update their resources in Question 2 of the I-Search Action Planner.

- Students will need several copies of the Note Sheets (Figure 5-1) as well as a copy of their Keyword Pathfinder (Figure 4-4), Wonderful Words chart (Figure 4-3), Resource Finder (Figure 5-9), and their Search Log (Figure 5-5).

- Several class sessions of thirty minutes to an hour depending on the age of the student are needed to research in the LMC. Some teachers find it effective to research a couple of days, meet back in the classroom to check student progress, and then return to the LMC for additional days of independent research.

Lesson Objective

Students will have opportunities to develop research and note-taking skills in the library with print, nonprint and online resources.

McREL Standards/Benchmarks—Language Arts, 4th ed.

- Standard 1: Uses the general skills and strategies of the writing process.

    1. Prewriting: Uses prewriting strategies to plan written work.

- Standard 4: Gathers and uses information for research purposes:

    2. Uses encyclopedias to gather information for research topics.

    3. Uses dictionaries to gather information for research topics.

4. Uses electronic media to gather information.

5. Uses keywords, guide words, alphabetical and numerical order, indices, cross-references, and letter volumes to find information for research topics.

6. Uses multiple representations of information.

7. Uses strategies to gather and record information for research topics.

8. Cites information sources.

AASL/AECT Information Literacy Standards

- Standard 1: The student who is information literate accesses information efficiently and effectively.

- Standard 3: The student who is information literate uses information accurately and creatively.

- Standard 4: The student who is an independent learner is information literate and pursues information related to personal interests.

- Standard 8: The student who contributes positively to the learning community and to society is information literate and practices ethical behavior in regard to information and information technology.

Research Sessions

- The first day, review Question 2 of the I-Search Action Plan with the students and discuss where the rest of their answers can be found. See Student I-Search Journal for completed student I-Search Plans.

- Explain to the students that they will be going to the LMC to find answers to their questions. Let the students know that they will also have opportunities to find other interesting facts about the unit and/or to find answers to additional questions they may have.

- Allow time for independent research.

- At the end of each research session, students need to complete a section of their Search Log. (See Figure 5-5.) The Search Log is a metacognitive tool that allows students to reflect, evaluate, and plan their search on a daily basis. Students record their thinking and research for use later in their research paper and project. The first line of the log represents the student's reflection of the day's activities where students record what was accomplished. The second line represents the self-evaluation of what was done. The third line gives students a chance to focus and plan the next day's activities.

Lesson 13: Summarize Notes	One to two 30–45-minute sessions	Teacher/Team and LMS

Upon completion of research in the library, students need to be shown how to summarize their notes.

Materials Needed

- Students' Note Sheets and I-Search Journals.
- Previously developed note sheet on transparency/poster/chart. (See Figure 5-2.)
- Information from interviews ready to be transferred to Note Sheets.
- Completed note sheet on transparency. (See Figure 5-10.)

Lesson Objective

Students will have the opportunity to develop summarization skills using their Note Sheets.

McREL Standards/Benchmarks—Language Arts, 4th ed.

- Standard 1: Uses the general skills and strategies of the writing process.
    1. Prewriting: Uses prewriting strategies to plan written work.

- Standard 4: Gathers and uses information for research purposes.
- Uses strategies to gather and record information for research topics (e.g., paraphrasing and summarizing information).

Completed Note Sheet

Name_____ Topic: Jackie Robinson

Question: Who was Jackie Robinson?

Notes:	Source:
Born Cairo, Georgia, 1919 Youngest five children Grandfather slave Father left family Family moved California Mother washed/ironed clothes make living p.	AOL@School. "Jackie Robinson" www.harcourtschool.com/activity/biographies/robinson/ April 20, 2004
Notes:	Source:
Played basketball, baseball, football, track Joined Army 1942 First African American play baseball Played Brooklyn Dodgers p.	KidsClick. "Jackie Robinson." http://library.thinkquest.org/10320/Robinson.htm April 20, 2004

Summary:

Jackie Robinson was an African American who was born in Cairo, Georgia, in 1919. He was the youngest of five children. His grandfather was a slave. His father left the family. The family moved to California where his mother washed and ironed clothes to make a living.

Jackie played baseball, basketball, football, and track. He joined the army in 1942. He played baseball and became the first African American to play in the major leagues. He played for the Brooklyn Dodgers.

Figure 5-10. Completed Note Sheets

• Uses strategies to compile information into written reports or summaries (e.g., drawing conclusions from relationship and patterns that emerge from data from different sources).

AASL/AECT Information Literacy Standards

• Standard 3: The student who is information literate uses information accurately and creatively.

Introduction

• Explain to the students that it is now important to put their notes in their own words. They are going to summarize the most important information they found to answer each question.

Guided Practice

• Use a note sheet that was developed in class to illustrate how to develop summaries. Think aloud about the process of putting the information from the notes into complete sentences.

• Model recording the first sentence for the students. Next, have students help you formulate the rest of the summary. (Duncan and Lockhart, 2000: 69)

• When the summary is written, go back and check your facts from the notes above. Make sure that all the information has been included. Remind students that they have summarized information from a variety of sources in order to answer the research question. Have students complete their matching Note Sheet. (See Figure 5-10.)

Individual Practice

• Break students into groups or pairs to work on the summary. Check for understanding by having groups share or by circulating among them.

• Differentiate the students by academic needs in order to finish summarizing the Note Sheets. Some students will be able to move along on their own. Others will still need to work with a partner. Lastly, others may need small-group instruction facilitated by the teacher in order to finish.

Closure/Input/Reflection

- Give students a choice of prompts to record in their I-Search Journal Reflections:

  1. I know I did my best work today because

     _____.

  2. I can make my work even better by

     _____.

  3. One thing I'm not sure of

     _____.

  4. Something I have learned that I can continue to use

     _____.

- Encourage students to share their reflections with their neighbor.

HOW WILL WE SHOW WHAT WE LEARNED?

INTRODUCTION

Students need, deserve, and must have opportunities to apply their learning in meaningful ways. Lessons to develop Summary Boards, a writing workshop, student-developed products based on the eight multiple intelligences, and presentation-skills lessons are all creative ways to apply information and are included in this chapter.

As mentioned earlier, students move a little closer to caring about their writing and how they will communicate their feelings and findings when they have an emotional investment in the unit of study. Using the I-Search process students will now have had opportunities to develop their questions and take their research in individual directions. They will also have a greater interest in the product if their choices include those that are complimentary to their particular interest and talents. Writing about their interests, developing products that illustrate those interests, and having the experience of presenting and sharing that product go a long way toward developing self-confident, lifelong learners. They are building skills to succeed both academically and socially.

The next lesson describes the introductory activities for creating the student Summary Board. This tool will allow students to organize information and draw conclusions from their research. It will also help students manage their information so that it is right at their fingertips when working on their presentations, papers, and products. Two file folders taped together in the middle form a convenient portfolio. Students will be able to use both sides and fold it up for easy storage.

Lesson 14: Construct Summary Boards	One 30–45-minute session	Teacher/Team/with LMS support

Materials Needed

- Picture or information book on unit topic
- Chart paper or poster board
- Colored markers/map pencils
- Two file folders for each student
- Tape for file folders
- Glue sticks
- Student scissors
- Student I-Search Journal (Focus on Figures 6-1 and 6-2)

Lesson Objective

Students will have the opportunity to sequence a story as preparation for organizing their Note Sheet summaries and developing their Summary Boards.

McREL Standards/Benchmarks—Language Arts, 4th ed.

- Standard 1: Uses the general skills and strategies of the writing process.
    1. Prewriting: Uses prewriting strategies to plan written work.
- Standard 4: Gathers and uses information for research purposes.
    7. Uses strategies to gather and record information for research topics (paraphrases and summarizes information).
    8. Uses strategies to compile information into written reports or summaries (e.g., draws conclusions from relationships and patterns that emerge from data from different sources).

AASL/AECT Information Literacy Standards

- Standard 3: The student who is information literate uses information accurately and creatively.

Anticipatory Set

- Reread and/or review a book on the unit topic that you have read previously (e.g., *Abuela* by Arthur Dorros for a unit on national heritage).
- Divide students into groups of three and assign the following roles:
    1. Materials Manager: Retrieves materials needed by the group
    2. Recorder: Writes down notes during brainstorming time
    3. Leader: Makes sure discussion is productive, the group is on task, and all members of the group are involved
- Assign each group a scene from the book the class has read.
- Have groups design and draw assigned scenes from the story on chart paper or poster board.
- Instruct groups to write a summary of their scene. Remind them to include a beginning, middle, and end.
- Invite students to arrange the drawings on the floor or tape them to the board in the order they appear in the story. Talk about first, last, after, and before.
- Students can walk from chart to chart sharing the story with a partner.
- To emphasize sequencing strategies, ask students a series of questions about the order of events. In response to the question "Did _____ happen before or after _____?" You might have the student stand above the event and point to the parts of the scene that provide the correct response.
- Create an all-class "Big Book" by putting all the charts/posters together.
- Talk to the students about the importance of keeping things in the right sequence. It helps the information and the story make sense.

(From *If the Shoe Fits: How to Develop Multiple Intelligences in the Classroom* by Carolyn Chapman. (c) 1993 by IRI/SkyLight Training and Publishing)

• Ask students:

1. What did you learn about story sequence?

2. How did walking through the story help?

3. What did you like best about your contribution to the whole story?

Reprinted by permission of LessonLab, a Pearson Education Company, www.lessonlab.com

Guided Practice

• Construct a Summary Board. Have students tape two file folders together, put their name in the upper right-hand corner, and prepare to put the summary boxes from their Note Sheets on their Summary Boards. See Figure 6-1.

• Students will apply what they learned about sequencing as they create their Summary Boards.

• Talk about the importance of putting things in the right sequence. We want the reader to understand the information and stay interested. Explain that they will be organizing the summary boxes from the Note Sheets in an order that makes sense and is interesting.

• Model each of the following steps to help students work through the activity using your own Note Sheets so that students will have a visual aid.

• Have students take their Note Sheets and cut out the summary boxes. Keep the other part of the Note Sheet in the pocket of the I-Search Journal since students will need the citations later when they create their bibliography.

• Have them spread out the summary boxes on their desks.

• Guide students through the process of grouping similar summaries together and deciding how to sequence the information.

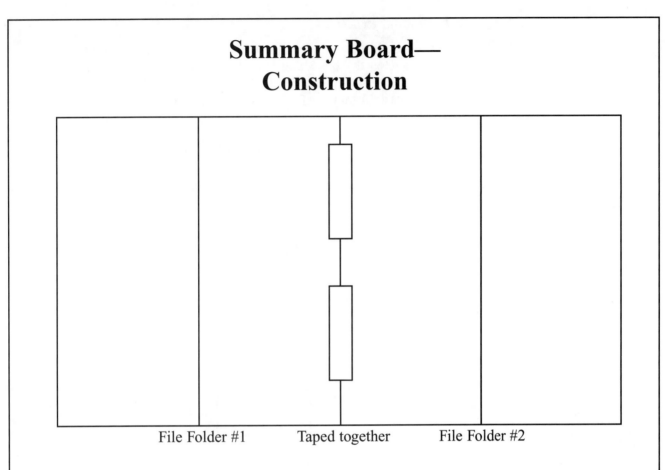

**Summary Board—
Construction**

File Folder #1   Taped together   File Folder #2

Directions:

- Construct a Summary Board.

- Tape two file folders together.

- Put your name in the upper right-hand corner.

- Place it in your I-Search Journal.

Figure 6-1. Summary Board—Construction

Individual Practice

- Explain that each student will receive a Summary Board. These boards will be used to organize and plan the rest of the research project. You can use a single file folder for four summaries or you can trim and tape two file folders together for up to eight summaries. Have students arrange the summaries on the board in order. They should leave room to the side of each summary. (See Figure 6-2.)

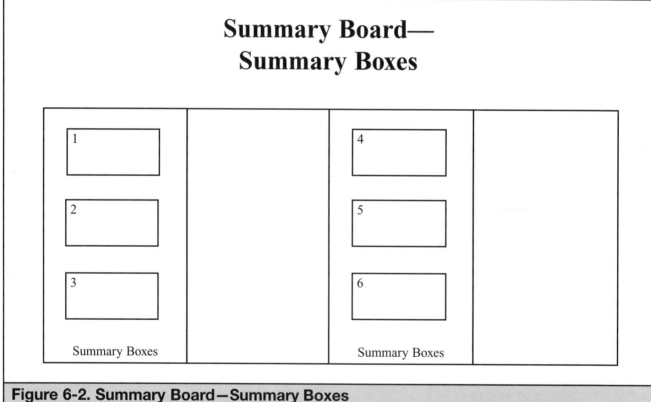

Summary Board—
Summary Boxes

Summary Boxes

Summary Boxes

Figure 6-2. Summary Board—Summary Boxes

- It is important to model the building of the summary board for students. As they are developing their boards have your own board to demonstrate how it is built.

- Monitor students as they group, sequence, and glue their summaries on the boards.

Closure

- I-Search Journal Reflection: How did sequencing the summary boxes on the Summary Boards affect the information? Discuss.

Ongoing Assessment

- Monitor students' understanding and application of the sequencing activity. Check Summary Boards and work with small groups as needed.

Lesson 15: Draw Conclusions	One 45–60-minute session	Teacher/Team or LMS

Introduction

- Lesson 15 provides an opportunity for students to reflect on their collected data in order to gain a better understanding of what they have gathered. The lesson will also serve as a prewriting activity. These prewriting activities are very important to the writer/researcher. They enable him or her to make observations and draw conclusions from the research as well as to reflect and prepare for the paper, product, and presentation.

Materials Needed

- Transparencies for "Tracks" pictures (See Figure 6-3)
- Teacher Summary Board with illustrated summaries
- Summary Board for each student
- Markers or map pencils
- I-Search Journal (Focus on Figure 6-4)

Lesson Objective

Students will reflect on the data that has been collected in order to gain a better understanding of what they have researched. Students will be able to draw conclusions from their research.

McREL Standards/Benchmarks—Language Arts, 4th ed.

- Standard 1: Uses the general skills and strategies of the writing process.
  1. Prewriting: Uses prewriting strategies to plan written work (groups' related ideas).

Tracks

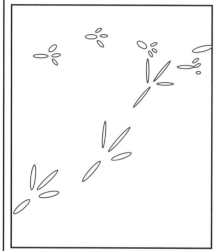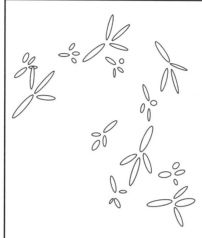

Source: *The Mindful School: How to Teach for Metacognitive Reflection*, by Robin Fogarty. © 1994 by IRI/SkyLight Training and Publishing. Reprinted by permission of LessonLab, a Pearson Education Company, www.lessonlab.com

Figure 6-3. Tracks

• Standard 4: Gathers and uses information for research purposes.

   7. Uses strategies to gather and record information for research topics.

   8. Uses strategies to compile information into written reports or summaries.

AASL/AECT Information Literacy Standards

• Standard 3: The student who is information literate uses information accurately and creatively.

Anticipatory Set

- Progressively show each frame of the three "Tracks" transparencies. (See Figure 6-3.) After each transparency have students list their observations in their I-Search Journals. For example, show frame one. Ask students to use the information and write down their observations of what they actually see. Repeat for the next two frames.

- At the end of the frames discuss with students what could be happening in the three scenes.

- After introducing the strategy relate it to real-world experiences. We have the tools to go beyond the given information and make meaning of data. Constructing new knowledge for ourselves helps us draw conclusions in real life.

- Some of these situations are:
  1. Drawing conclusions about people's moods from their body language, facial expressions, or tone of voice.
  2. Drawing conclusions about a setting of a story from the images in our minds.

- To continue to practice the skill of drawing conclusions, show students a thought-provoking picture about the unit of study. For example, pictures from the book *Immigrant Kids*, by Russell Freedman, is a good source of pictures to use to draw conclusions about a person's mood.

- Explain that the first step to drawing conclusions is making and recording observations.

- Once students have recorded their observations have them read through their notes. These should be just the facts they see. When they are satisfied with their observations they should draw conclusions about what is going on in the picture.

(From *The Mindful School: How to Teach for Metacognitive Reflection*, by Robin Fogarty. (c) 1994 by IRI/SkyLight Training and Publishing. Reprinted by permission of LessonLab, a Pearson Education Company, *www.lessonlab.com*.)

Guided Practice

- Go over the major components of how to draw conclusions:

    1. Observation of facts

    2. Putting together the facts

    3. Visualization of what could be happening or what the information means based on the facts

- Review with students that they can use this skill in everyday life by gathering data and drawing conclusions about how people feel, interpreting charts and graphs, and being observant of information as they read and research. Share with the students that they will be using this skill when they work on their Summary Boards. This strategy will help them make meaning of their research.

- Model the following activities and follow with individual practice:

    1. Read your first summary.

    2. Draw pictures, charts, and/or graphs to draw conclusions and make meaning of the summary. The drawings do not have to be in finished form because this is a first draft.

    3. Information in the summary boxes that goes together may be combined for one picture, graph, or chart. (See Figure 6-4.)

    4. Once the activity has been modeled have children begin working on their own Summary Boards. Have students work together as they read their summaries, interpret information, and create graphs, sketches, and charts. This activity generates a lot of discussion and reflection.

Closure

- At the conclusion of this activity allow students to share and discuss their work. Ask students to describe their choice of picture or graph.

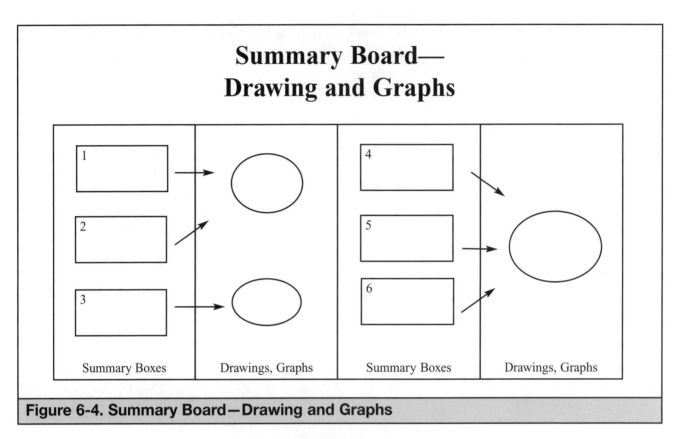

Figure 6-4. Summary Board—Drawing and Graphs

Ongoing Assessment

- Circulate and check for understanding. Meet with small groups or individuals to adjust and/or reteach.

Lesson 16: Develop Main Idea	One 45–60-minute session	Teacher/Team or LMS

Materials Needed

- Picture book or information book on unit topic
- Graphic to symbolize unit of study and to illustrate main idea
- Summary Boards for each student
- Teacher example of Summary Board
- Student I-Search Journal (Focus on Figures 6-5 and 6-6)

Lesson Objective

Students will be able to develop a main idea with supporting facts for their research.

McREL Standards/Benchmarks—Language Arts, 4th ed.

- Standard 1: Uses the general skills and strategies of the writing process.

    1. Prewriting: Uses prewriting strategies to plan written work (e.g., uses graphic organizers).

- Standard 7: Uses reading skills and strategies to understand and interpret a variety of informational texts.

    5. Summarizes and paraphrases information in texts (e.g., includes the main idea and supporting facts of a reading selection).

AASL/AECT Information Literacy Standards

- Standard 3: The student who is information literate uses information accurately and creatively.

Anticipatory Set

- Using the "Careful Reader" strategies found in Figure 4-1 and in the student I-Search Journal, read a book on the unit topic to the students. *The Best Town in the World*, a poem in book form by Byrd Baylor, is a great book for this activity.

Discuss and celebrate the book.

- When the students are ready to move on to the skill lesson, discuss with them what the main idea of a story is:

Important details answer the questions who, what, when, where, why and how. The main idea is the most important idea in a story or paragraph that can be stated in one sentence. If you put the main idea and the important details together in your own words, you are creating a summary. (Texas Assessment of Knowledge and Skills Study Guide, Grade 3, 2003: 30)

- Use a graph or picture that symbolizes the unit of study or symbolizes the book shared with the students. For example, for a unit on the National Heritage a flag graphic could be used. See Figure 6-5.

Main Idea Flag Graphic

Figure 6-5. Main Idea Flag Graphic

- Ask students for detailed summaries of what the story is about and record them on the body of the flag. Next, determine the main idea from the supporting facts and record it in the square on the flag. Explain that the supporting statements hold up the main idea.

- Let students know that the next step will be to come up with a main idea for their research. They will use their Summary Boards to do this.

Guided Practice

- Review what was learned about main idea. Explain to the students that they will review the Summary Boards for the details of their research. They will then come up with a main idea that may also be used as an introduction for the research paper.

Individual/Group Practice

- Have students work in groups or individually to create the main idea of their research. Groups will depend on the ability of your students.
- Have students write the main idea on the back of their Summary Boards. (See Figure 6-6.) They will be able to use their main idea statements for their products, papers, and presentations.

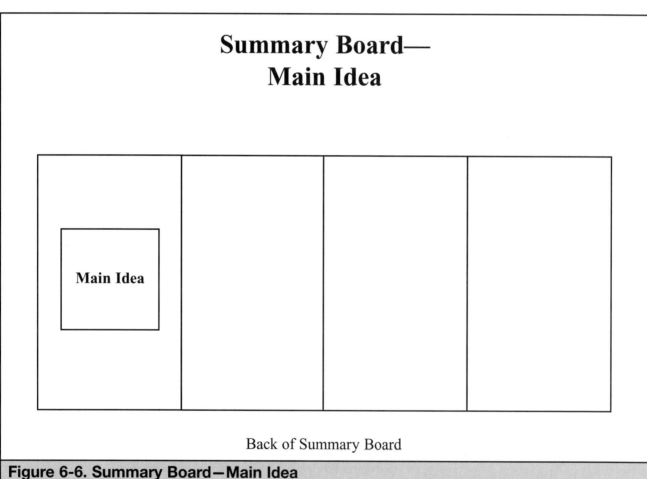

Summary Board—
Main Idea

Main Idea

Back of Summary Board

Figure 6-6. Summary Board—Main Idea

- This can be is a complicated task for students. This is even more true if they have not had much practice. This entire activity may need to be modeled for the whole class or small groups of students who are struggling.

Closure/Input/Reflection

- Closure Questions and Journal Reflection
    1. What did we accomplish by doing what we just did?
    2. Why did we do what we did?
    3. How might you be able to use what we did?
- Debrief in small groups or as a class.

Lesson 17: List Sources	One 30–45-minute session	LMS or Teacher/Team

Materials Needed

- I-Search Journals
- Bibliographic information from Note Sheets
- Glue sticks
- Student scissors
- Summary Boards
- Teacher example of completed Summary Boards or Note Sheets with bibliographic information
- Student I-Search Journals (focus on bibliography portion of Note Sheets)

Lesson Objective

Students will be able to alphabetize the citations for their research paper and create their bibliography or source list.

McREL Standards/Benchmarks—Language Arts, 4th ed.

- Standard 1: Uses the general skills and strategies of the writing process.
    1. Prewriting: Uses prewriting strategies to plan written work.
- Standard 4: Gathers and uses information for research purposes.
    9. Cites information sources.

AASL/AECT Information Literacy Standards

- Standard 3: The student who is information literate uses information accurately and creatively.

Guided Practice

- Explain that it is important to show where we find the information we use. This also helps others locate the information we used in order to learn more about the topic.
- Model the following process:
    1. Take the source section of the Note Sheets and cut them apart.
    2. Circle the author's last name or publisher.
    3. Stack or sort the source cards in alphabetical order by the last name. Review alphabetical order with students.
    4. Glue the source cards in alphabetical order to the back of the summary board.
    5. Students will use this information to record their bibliography in final form as part of their research paper. (See Figure 6-7.)

Closure/Input/Reflection

- Have students check one another's projects in small groups in order to determine if everyone arranged the sources in alphabetical order.

Lesson 18: Summarize the Search	One to two 30–45-minute sessions	Teacher/Team with LMS support

Materials Needed

- Student Search Logs from I-Search Journals (See Figures 6-9 and 6-11.)
- Search Summary graphic for each student
- Transparency for Search Summary graphic
- Student and teacher Summary Boards
- Teacher example of Search Log (See Figure 6-8.)

Summary Board—Bibliography

			Bibliography
Main Idea			A B C D

Figure 6-7. Summary Board—Bibliography

Lesson Objective

Students will have the opportunity to use their skills of summarization while summarizing the story of their "search" with a graphic organizer.

McREL Standards/Benchmarks—Language Arts, 4th edition

- Standard 1: Uses the general skills and strategies of the writing process.
    1. Prewriting: Uses prewriting strategies to plan written work (e.g., uses graphic organizers).
- Standard 4: Gathers and uses information for research purposes.
    10. Uses strategies to compile information into written reports or summaries (e.g., draws conclusions from relationships and patterns that emerge from data from different sources).

AASL/AECT Information Literacy Standards

- Standard 3: The student who is information literate uses information accurately and creatively.

Anticipatory Set

- Introduce the lesson by reflecting on the variety of activities the class has been involved in while researching. The story of their search is important to share because students can learn from others' processes and they can celebrate their accomplishments. Today's activities will help with the paper and presentation portion of the unit.

- Remind them that summary is not the same as main idea. A summary includes the most important points that someone needs to know to understand the whole story while the main idea is the single most important idea in the story.

- Tell them that they are going to create a summary of their research process using a graphic organizer.

Guided Practice

- Use the Search Logs to gather information for the Search Summary. (See Figure 6-8.)
- Model the activity:
  - Circle "What did I accomplish today?" section of the Search Log and review.
  - Use the Search Summary graphic to write "treasure words" as defined by Barbara Jansen for what happened in the beginning, middle, and end of the research. (See Figure 6-9.)
  - Model recording a summary of the search. (See Figure 6-10.)
  - Paste the Search Summary to the back of the Summary Board. (See Figure 6-11.)

Individual/Group Practice

- Have students work individually and/or in small groups to develop their own Search Summaries.
- Have students paste their Search Summaries on their Summary Boards.

Search Log—Completed

Date: October 20, 2004

How have I done so far? I have found articles in the *World Book Encyclopedia* and *Webster's Biographical Dictionary* on Jackie Robinson.

What quality of work have I done? Pretty good.

What do I need to do next? Find a simple biography on Jackie Robinson.

Date: October 21, 2004

What have I accomplished so far? I found the biography, *Jackie Robinson*, by Harvey Fromm and used the *African American Encyclopedia*.

What quality of work have I done? Good.

What do I need to do next? Use the Internet.

Date: October 22, 2004

What have I accomplished so far? I found a long article on Yahooligans about Jackie Robinson as a baseball player.

What quality of work have I done? Very good.

What do I need to do next? Finish taking notes from the Internet article.

Figure 6-8. Search Log—Completed

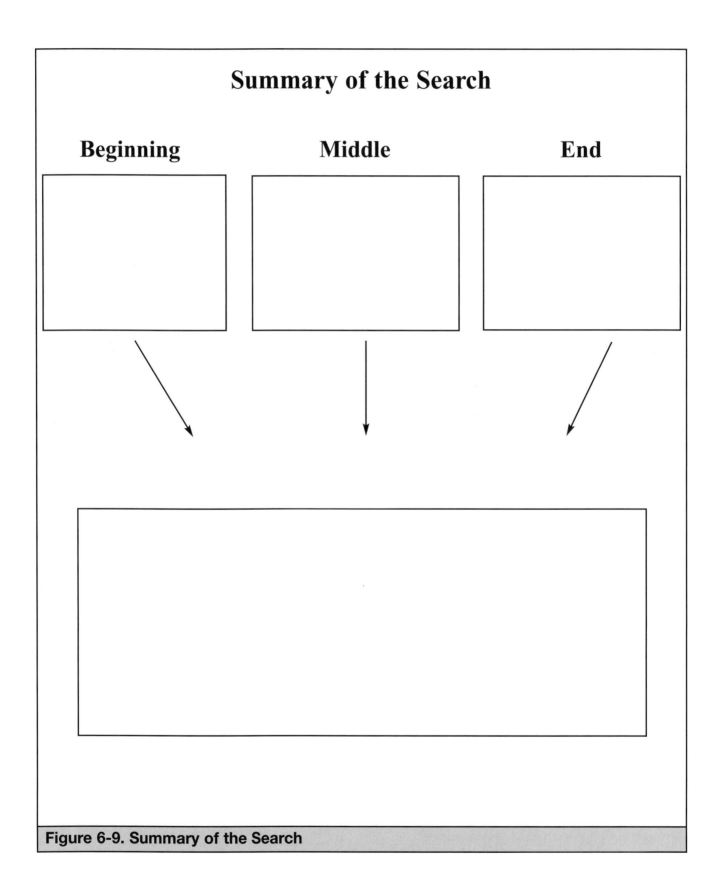

Figure 6-9. Summary of the Search

Summary of the Search—Completed

Beginning

I chose Jackie Robinson to research. I used the *World Book Encyclopedia* and the *Webster's Biographical Dictionary* to find information.

Middle

Next, I checked out a biography, *Jackie Robinson*, by Harvey Fromm, and used the *African American Encyclopedia*.

End

Last, I searched the Internet and found an article on Jackie Robinson and his baseball career on Yahooligans.

My search for information about Jackie Robinson began with the *World Book Encyclopedia* and *Webster's Biographical Dictionary*. I did a good job using them but I felt that I needed to understand Jackie Robinson better so I read his biography by Henry Fromm. That really helped. After that I used the Internet to find information about him and his baseball career.

Figure 6-10. Summary of the Search—Completed

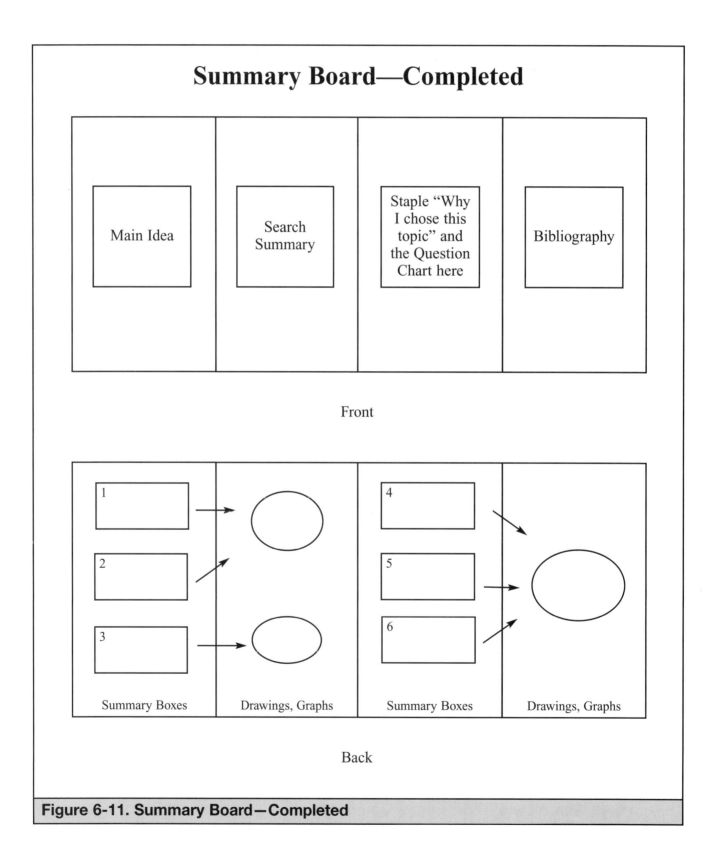

Figure 6-11. Summary Board—Completed

Closure/Input/Reflection

- To complete the Summary Boards students need to attach their first draft of "Why I Chose" and the question chart from their I-Search Journals. Students simply staple both pages on the last blank section of the Summary Board. Students will now use their Summary Boards to help them write their research papers and develop their products. Review components of the Summary Board (e.g., main idea, Search Summary, "Why I Chose This Topic" writing assignment, question chart, summary boxes, and bibliography).

Ongoing Assessment

- Check students' Summary Boards for completion.

USING THE SUMMARY BOARD

It is now time to use the Summary Board to write the paper. We have studied the work of Lucy Calkins, Shelly Hawayne, Nancy Atwell, Donald Graves, and Vicki Spandle among many others. These outstanding writing experts have taught us about the writing process and effective traits of writing. Our goal is to integrate many of those writing practices into the I-Search Unit. We have attempted to provide some ideas for taking the paper through the writing process while citing examples of activities that you can use to teach effective traits of writing. You may be able to integrate the writing of the paper into your already existing writing workshop and/or simply build on the effective traits of writing you have been working on all year. This may be a first run for others. In either instance use what you are comfortable with and that for which your students are ready. This section will not be organized with specific lessons, but will give you information and ideas to organize lessons based on the skill level of your students.

Lesson 19: Organize Writing Workshop	Two to three 45–60-minute sessions	Teacher/Team Support from LMS

Materials Needed

- Summary Boards for each student
- Blank notebook paper and pencils
- Student I-Search Journals (See Figures 6-12 and 6-13)

- Poster of writing process. See Figure 6-12.
- Chart paper
- Highlighters
- Access to a word processor

Writing Process

Prewriting

Drafting

Revising and editing

Final copy

Figure 6-12. Writing Process

Lesson Objective

Students will have an opportunity to write an I-Search paper based on their research.

McREL Standards/Benchmarks—Language Arts, 4th ed.

- Standard 1: Uses the general skills and strategies of the writing process.

    2. Drafting and Revising: Uses strategies to draft and revise written work.

3. Editing and Publishing: Uses strategies to edit and publish written work.

4. Evaluates own and others' writing.

5. Uses strategies to write for different audiences.

6. Uses strategies to write for a variety of purposes.

7. Writes expository compositions (i.e., identifies and stays on the topic; develops the topic with simple details, examples, and explanations; excludes extraneous and inappropriate information; uses structures such as cause and effect, chronology, similarities and differences; uses several sources of information; and uses a concluding statement).

• Standard 2: Uses the stylistic and rhetorical aspects of writing

1. Uses descriptive language that clarifies and enhances ideas.

2. Uses paragraph form in writing.

3. Uses a variety of sentence structures in writing.

AASL/AECT Information Literacy Standards

• Standard 3: The student who is information literate uses information accurately and creatively.

• Standard 5: The student who is an independent learner is information literate and appreciates literature and other creative expressions of information.

Guided Practice

The writing process includes 1) prewriting, 2) drafting, 3) revising and editing and 4) final copy activities. Students need to understand these components and that you will be guiding the research through this writing process. (See Figure 6-12.)

1. Prewriting:

Much of the prewriting has been completed. Students have researched and reflected on their work.

2. Drafting:

Students have also completed a majority of their first draft with their summary boxes, question chart, Search Summary, and "Why I Chose This Topic?" writing assignment. They have organized their Summary Boards for easy use of writing the second draft. When students write or type their second draft, they have the opportunity to organize the paper into the I-Search format:

- Title
- Why I chose this topic (Why I Chose This Topic?)
- What I knew before I started (First column of question chart)
- The Search (Search Summary)
- What I learned (Summary Boards)
- Bibliography (Resource List)

Encourage students to write in first person and to communicate excitement about their topic as they are putting their information together for their second draft. Instruct them to make it interesting so that the people reading their papers will want to keep reading to learn more about them as the author and about the subject they are writing about. (Macrorie, 1988) The best way to communicate these expectations is to model the process for them and to give them good examples of great writing. More ideas on these examples are in the next section.

3. Revising and editing:

Following are activities using traits of writing that you may use to teach the revision and editing process. Typically, these traits are not taught all at once. They become a process and practice of the class-room and are built upon through daily writing, reflection, and discovery. (Spandel, 2001) Vicki Spandel, in *Creating Writers* has incredible ideas, activities, and research on the 'Six Traits of Writing' that will strengthen your students' research papers. They are:

Trait 1: Ideas

a. Teach students to "write with detail, a sharp eye, clarity and focus and separate the interesting from the mundane." (Spandel, 2001: 160) An activity to demonstrate this is to highlight the details:

> In any given piece of writing, some details catch your eye or imagination. Some you hardly notice. Pull a piece from any literature you and your students are studying; it should be at least a half page long, but no more than two. Ask students to work with a partner to highlight in yellow those details that capture their imagination. Discuss results as a class to see how closely students agree. Talk about what makes some details more important or interesting than others. Do certain details appeal to a certain audience? How much should writers think about this? (Spandel, 2001: 160)

Always model these activities using your own writing and thinking aloud while you write.

b. Students can then begin to read their second drafts for interesting ideas:

- Is the topic narrow and manageable?
- Is the main idea supported with accurate details?
- Does the piece include fresh and original ideas?
- Does the writer seem to be writing from experience or knowledge?

    (NWREL, 2001: 2)

Monitor and discuss with students to check for understanding.

c. Have students read their drafts for interesting details and go through the four questions (listed in number 2, above). You may also have students partner up and read and work on their drafts with one another.

d. Be sure the paper is in first person throughout.

Trait 2: Organization

Organization includes focusing on leads, sequencing, transitions, and conclusions. As stated earlier, reading nonfiction aloud to students will help with their understanding of nonfiction text, but will also aid in their writing of nonfiction.

"Reading front page articles, reviews, personal essays, excerpts from well-written nonfiction journals (e.g., *Discover Magazine, Dig, Ranger Rick*) and editorials lend validity to forms of writing that may not be as familiar as the story. ..." (Spandel, 2001: 197) Students need to focus on leads, sequencing, transitions, and conclusions. In addition to modeling these techniques you can utilize the following activities:

a. Leads

- Compare different leads from informational text.

- Have students review their information and select intriguing details on which to base a lead. (Spandel, 2001: 201)

- Have them also review the main idea from their summary boards to develop a lead.

- Remember to make sure the lead matches the first person style of the paper.

b. Transitions

- "Choose a published piece with strong transitions (science and wildlife journals are excellent sources), and rewrite it with all transitional phrases missing. Ask students to fill in transitional words and phrases that make sense." (Spandel, 2001: 201)

- Brainstorm a list of good transitional words and phrases: *however, in a while, therefore, next, because of that, in fact, on the other hand, to tell the truth, for example, nevertheless, I also learned,* and so forth. Make a poster from which student writers can "borrow" when they need a way to link ideas. Teacher and students can both add to the poster. (Spandel, 2001: 201–202)

- Have students use their transition skills to review their drafts for strong transitions. Students may work in pairs and small groups while you conference and check for understanding.

c. Sequencing

The organizational skill of sequencing was addressed when the summary boxes were attached to the Summary Boards and when students wrote their second drafts.

d. Conclusion

Developing an interesting conclusion helps to conclude the writing with a sense of completeness. Following are examples of lessons and ideas to help students with conclusions:

• Compare conclusions from informational texts.

• "Ask students to write three to five possible endings to pieces they are working on and to share these possibilities in writing groups. Join the fun, writing potential conclusions for your own writing." (Spandel, 2001: 202)

• Have students choose or consolidate their best conclusion and add it to their draft. Monitor the groups and check conclusions for understanding.

• Keep in mind that the conclusions should match the first-person style.

Trait 3: Voice

When a paper has voice "the writer speaks directly to the reader in a way that is individual and engaging." (NWREL, 2004: 4) Voice has a prominent place in the I-Search paper. Students have connected with their subject with individual questions and individual interest. Do not merely encourage this excitement and individuality, but nurture it as well. Following are some examples of strategies to teach voice.

• "Read aloud lots of pieces that have voice. Search everywhere: novels, picture books, anthologies, greeting cards, brochures, menus, movie reviews, screen plays, letters, keep reading, keep asking, what gives this voice? What is Voice?" (Spandel, 2001: 203)

• Books that illustrate voice and also have a National Heritage theme include: *Brother Eagle, Sister Sky* by Chief Seattle; *Tar Beach* by Faith Ringgold; *This Land is My Land* by George Littlechild; and *Feliciana Feydra Le Roux* by Tynia Thamassie.

• Model the above activities with your own writing. You can show a before and after draft to show how powerful adding voice can be.

- First-person writing enhances the power of voice and helps to create an engaging report.

Trait 4: Word Choice

When writing has good word choice the "words convey the intended message in a precise, interesting, and natural way. The words are powerful and engaging." (NWREL, 2004: 5) Following are ideas for implementing word choice strategies:

- "Brainstorm a list of 'tired' words and phrases that needs a long (permanent?) rest such as fun (as an adjective), awesome, great, nice, bad (meaning good), way cool, grand and super. For each tired word or expression, also brainstorm as many different 'ways to say it' as you can think of. Create word walls for students to reference and keep adding to the list." (Spandel, 2001: 206)

- Model this process by identifying four to five tired words in your writing. Brainstorm with the class to find better words. Have students do the same with their drafts. Students may work in pairs or small groups as you monitor and help. This is also a good opportunity to introduce or reinforce the proper way to use a thesaurus.

Trait 5: Fluency

When writing has fluency it has "an easy flow, rhythm, and cadence. Sentences are well built, with strong and varied structure that invites expressive oral reading." (NWREL, 2001: 6) Following is a series of questions and suggestions to model for students to implement for their second drafts:

a. Do sentences begin in different ways?

b. Do sentences vary in length and structure?

c. Can the reader move with ease from one sentence to the next?

d. Does the writing have a natural flow when read aloud?

Conference with individuals and small groups as they work through these fluency strategies.

Trait 6: Conventions

Writing conventions include spelling, grammar, paragraph development, capitalization, and punctuation. Experts such as Spandel (2001) encourage us to avoid asking students to correct every single problem rather than edit one or two so that they are not overwhelmed. Depending on your students' level and experience with editing, model using the editing marks and then have students work on their drafts. Have conferences with students as they work with conventions and editing marks. (See Figure 6-13.)

4   Final Copy Activities:

a.   Students have organized their paper to include: Why I Chose This Topic? with a lead sentence, What I Knew Before I Started, The Search, and What I Learned with a nice conclusion.

Revising and Editing

(-) Put one line through things you want to take out.

(^) Use a caret to add letters, words, and/or sentences.

◯   Circle words that are misspelled.

(≡) Put three lines under letters that need to be capitalized.

(.) (?) (!) Add any punctuation that is missing.

(/) Put a slash through any letters that need to be lower case.

Figure 6-13. Revising and Editing

b. They have taken their research through prewriting, draft, and revision and editing. They are now ready to write their final copy. Students need to have time to reflect and complete this copy.

c. They need to develop their bibliography or list of sources from their Summary Boards.

d. During this process they may use their writing skills to make additional improvements to their writing.

e. Encourage students to read aloud their final copy for any revisions or edits in preparation for their presentation.

f. Review the I-Search paper rubric in order to remind students of the grading criteria. (See Figure 7-2.)

Lesson 20: Produce Products, Make Presentations, and Create Celebrations	Four to five 45–60-minute sessions	Teacher/Team/LMS

Materials Needed

- Product contract and rubric for each student
- List of products posted (Figure 6-14)
- I-Search Action Plan for each student
- Presentation forms for each student
- Student I-Search Journal—Summary Board, copy of product contract, product rubric, copy of I-Search paper, letter to parents
- Tips to help parents facilitate the student project

Lesson Objective

Students will have the opportunity to develop a product to illustrate their research findings and I-Search paper and present those discoveries to their class.

McREL Standards/Benchmarks—Language Arts, 4th ed.

- Standard 4: Gathers and uses information for research purposes.

    8. Uses strategies to compile information into written reports or summaries (e.g., uses appropriate visual aids and media).

- Standard 8: Uses listening and speaking strategies for different purposes.

    1. Uses strategies to convey a clear main point when speaking.

    2. Uses level-appropriate vocabulary in speech.

    3. Makes basic oral presentation to class (e.g., incorporates visual aids or props).

    4. Uses a variety of nonverbal communication skills (e.g., eye contact, gestures, facial expressions).

    5. Uses a variety of verbal communication skills (e.g., projection, tone, volume, rate, articulation, pace).

    6. Organizes ideas for oral presentations (e.g., uses an introduction and conclusion; uses notes or other aids; organizes ideas around major points, in sequence, or chronologically; uses traditional structure such as cause and effect, similarity and difference, posing and answering a question; uses details and examples of anecdotes to clarify information).

    7. Understands the main ideas and supporting details in spoken texts (e.g., presentations by peers or speakers).

AASL/AECT Information Literacy Standards

- Standard 5: The student who is an independent learner is information literate and appreciates literature and other creative expressions of information.

- Standard 7: The student who contributes positively to the learning community and to society is information literate and recognizes the importance of information to a democratic society.

Introduction

Developing products to demonstrate learning and sharing that information through presentations to their peers culminates the I-Search Unit experience. This helps students become active, lifelong learners who can:

> figure things out by themselves; generate their own examples; trust their own hypotheses; demonstrate their own skills; assess their own competencies; determine the qualities of their efforts; apply what they have learned to new situations; and teach others what they have learned. (Silver, Strong, Perin, 2001: 1)

This lesson is actually a series of activities that would more appropriately be called a Presentation Workshop. It includes:

Product Presentation Steps

1. Producing a product
2. Using a rubric
3. Completing product at home
4. Participating in presentation lessons
5. Unit celebration/student presentation
6. Developing Listening skills
7. Celebrating the person on stage

PRODUCING A PRODUCT

- During the unit introduction, students were given a choice of a product that they could create as part of the I-Search Action Plan. They took the product contract home in order to make their parents aware of the I-Search process and expectations.
- As the unit progressed, students may have changed their minds about how to best illustrate their research. They may have decided that a multimedia presentation would explain what they learned better than a song or rap.

• They should make a final decision on the product they will produce to show what they have learned at this time. See Figure 6-14 for a list of products.

USING A RUBRIC

• There should be a rubric for each product—the I-Search paper and the presentation. Rubrics developed collaboratively by student and teacher are powerful. They give students ownership of their learning and assessment. As a result, students are more likely to

Multiple Intelligence-Based Products

Multiple Intelligences	Products
• Musical Rhythmic ⟶	• Create a song, rap, musical, or jingle
• Visual Spatial ⟶	• Poster, brochure, mural, maps, and videos
• *Intrapersonal ⟶	• I-Search Journal
• Bodily Kinesthetic ⟶	• Create a drama, role-play, mime or dance
• Interpersonal ⟶	• Interviews, questionnaires, or people searches
• Logical Mathematical ⟶	• Charts, graphs, multimedia presentations
• Naturalistic ⟶	• Photographic display, dioramas, video tape scenes from nature
• *Verbal Linguistic ⟶	• I-Search paper/presentation
*Required for all students	Students have choice of unmarked products

Source: From *Multiple Intelligence Approaches to Assessment: Solving the Assessment Conundrum*, 1999, by David Lazear, Zephyr Press (www.zephyrpress.com).

Figure 6-14. Multiple Intelligence-Based Products

understand and follow the guidelines for a good product. See Chapter 7 for more information on developing rubrics.

- Students must know and understand the criteria for evaluation of their products before they begin work on them. Make copies of the rubrics for students to use while they are creating their I-Search products. This allows students to choose the level of criteria they wish to work toward while they are constructing their product.

Completing Products at Home

- Products may be completed at home or in the classroom. It has been our experience that it is a better use of instructional time if the product is completed at home. This also allows the family to become involved in the process. Comments from our students indicate that special experiences with family members have resulted from working together on the products.

- Send home the Summary Board, I-Search paper, and appropriate product rubric if the products are done at home. A copy of the contract signed at the beginning of the unit and a letter to parents should go home with the I-Search packet. The letter should include tips to help parents facilitate the project.

- This is an incredible opportunity for parents and children to work together and enjoy one another. Perfection is not a requirement; authentic work by the student is.

Presentation Lessons

- Communication skills and strategies should be introduced as early as possible in the year. Students are then able to build on the skills throughout the year in many different ways. The more experience they have using their skills, the more opportunity they will have to grow, learn, and have confidence in front of an audience.

- Learning to speak in front of a group can begin at an early age. In his book, *Listening and Speaking: Activities for Grades 2–3,* Bob Krech provides a literature link to public speaking with the book *Arthur Meets the President*, by Marc Brown,

- Another literature link to public speaking is the book *Ruby Mae Has Something to Say,* by David Small. Books such as these can trigger a discussion on the fear of speaking in public. It is important to prepare students to do their best when they present their I-Search papers and products. Comments from our students through the years have indicated that this is a source of anxiety for them.

- Communication lessons that teach eye contact, diction and volume, posture and gestures, and organization are presented in our first book, *I-Search, You Search, We All Learn to Research.*

- As students organize their presentations have them include an "attention getter" lead statement, the story of their search, a description of the project facts they learned, and a nice closing statement.

- Students can organize their presentation on note cards using their Summary Boards and completed I-Search papers. You can work with students to organize their presentations and to improve presentation skills while they are completing the projects at home.

Unit Celebrations/Student Presentations

- Student presentations are an important component of the Unit Celebration. Celebrations depend on the theme of the unit. A Folklore Festival with music, pictures, artifacts, food, and games from the different regions of the country is a natural choice for a National Heritage unit.

- The focus, though, should be on the student presentations. It is important to place value on this experience by inviting parents and friends to share in the celebration. The presentations may be spread over two or three days, or they may be presented all in one day. Have a sign-up sheet for parents and teachers to come in order to avoid having too many visitors at once or none at all.

Listening Skills

- Listening skills are as important as presentation skills and are part of the instructional standards. Before the presentations begin, discuss audience etiquette. Students should listen with their whole body. For example, they need to make eye contact and listen to what the speaker is really saying.

- Provide each audience member with a presentation chart. (See Figure 6-15.) Assess each student's listening skills by having everyone take notes after each person presents. This also gives students something to do between presentations as presenters take down and set up their projects.

Celebrating the Person on Stage

- Students have spent many weeks on their project and have become experts on their topics. Let them answer questions about their learning and their projects.

- At the conclusion of the presentations, the projects and papers can be displayed for the whole school to see.

- Be sure to get pictures of the students with their projects. They can put the pictures on the cover sheets of their papers or attach them to their projects and put them in their I-Search Journal when the projects are no longer displayed. As a result, others will be able to put a face with each project and continue to celebrate your community of learners!

Presenter _____**Topic**_____

What I learned:

_____

Presenter _____**Topic**_____

What I learned:

_____

Presenter _____**Topic**_____

What I learned:

Figure 6-15. Presentations

7 HOW WILL WE KNOW WE DID A GOOD JOB?

Assessments	Ongoing and one day at end of unit	Teacher/Team/LMS

INTRODUCTION

Carol Ann Tomlinson maintains, "To truly measure achievement, grading practices should grow from a philosophy of teaching and learning that respects student differences and reflects individual growth." (Tomlinson, 2001: 12) She explains that teachers who want to help all students succeed in academically diverse classrooms often tell her, "I know I'm losing students when I teach as though they were all alike. I want to learn to be a more flexible teacher so that I can reach more of them. But even if I could figure out how to do that, how would I grade them?" (Tomlinson, 2001: 12) This, too, has been a concern on the part of teachers and LMS in relation to I-Search Units. They need to know that opportunities for assessment and grades equal the time investment. Grades are important for a variety of reasons.

Robert Marzano, in his book, *Transforming Classroom Grading,* quotes John Hattie as asserting, "the most powerful single innovation that enhances achievement is feedback. The simplest prescription for improving education must be "dollops of feedback." Thus, "the most important purpose for grades is to provide information or feedback to students and parents." (Hatti, quoted in Marzano, 2000: 23) This is sometimes difficult in a society where the emphasis on tests is accountability. Our challenge is both to provide students the opportunity to experience authentic assessment with the needed feedback and to prepare them to achieve on the standardized tests. It is possible to do both. Students who experience authentic assessment in a variety of situations will be more than prepared to do well on the state tests. Sylwester is a proponent of this belief as well. He asserts that "continuous informal evaluations that focus more on what we can do than on what we cannot do create a necessary climate of positive social feedback." (Sylwester, 2000: 28)

The I-Search Unit process lends itself to a variety of ongoing assessment and evaluation tools for teachers and students to receive feedback. Student assessments include primary trait rubrics for the research paper, products, and presentation, an I-Search Journal portfolio, and a self-evaluation. Teacher assessments include the teacher/librarian collaborative-unit assessment and a standards-based grade sheet that is correlated to the McREL Standards/Benchmarks. See Figure 7-1.

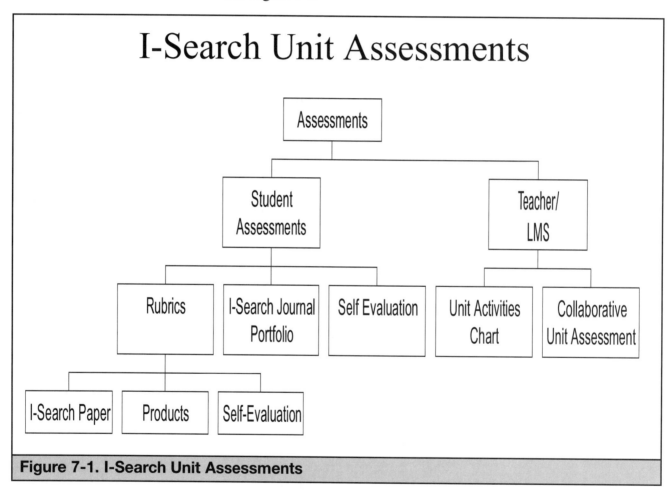

I-Search Unit Assessments

Figure 7-1. I-Search Unit Assessments

DETERMINE STUDENT ASSESSMENTS

RUBRICS

We use the primary trait rubrics in this book as we did in, *I-Search, You Search, We All Learn to Research*. The primary trait rubrics focus on a particular trait (Rogers, Ludington and Graham, 1998). When we focus on the characteristics of a good oral speech or an effective multimedia presentation, we are using a primary trait rubric. The convenient aspect of this type of rubric is that a general rubric can be developed and then modified to create a series of different primary trait rubrics (Rogers, Ludington and Graham, 1998). We use the same rubric format for the I-Search paper, presentation, and projects. The traits are changed for each format.

"How do I create a rubric that ensures student ownership?" is also a question people ask us frequently. In their book, *Motivation and Learning,* Rogers, Ludington, and Graham discuss how to develop primary trait rubrics with students. There is also a lesson in *I-Search, You Search, We All Learn to Research* about developing primary trait rubrics. Developing rubrics in this manner allows students to be a part of the development and assessment process. The learning becomes directed and accountability more meaningful. When students have ownership of their learning, evaluation and assessment allow them to play an integral role in the learning process and to be meaningful partners. Examples of these rubrics are found in Figures 7-2, 7-3, and 7-4.

Other kinds of rubrics may be found online at:

1. Kathy Schrock's Web site—http://school.discovery .com/schrockguide/assess.html.

   This site references student Web page rubrics, subject-specific rubrics, and general rubrics for students, as well as technology-skills rubrics for educators.

2. RubricBuilder—www.landmark-project.com/ classweb/tools/rubric_builder.php.

3. Rubistar—http://rubistar.4teachers.org/index.php.

4. TEACH-NOLOGY—www.teach-nology.com/web _tools/rubrics.

I-SEARCH JOURNAL PORTFOLIO OR PERFORMANCE CHECKLIST

Each student will be responsible for compiling an I-Search Journal Portfolio as the unit progresses. "Portfolio assessments are another excellent vehicle for encouraging the self-examination in students that enhances their self-concept and self-esteem." (Sylwester, 2000: 61) Students will have multiple opportunities to add to their journal/portfolio. It will be a valuable record of their work throughout the unit. Students will complete the I-Search Journal Portfolio checklist upon the completion of the unit. (See Figure 7-5.)

I-Search Paper Rubric

Rating	Conventions	Voice	Ideas/ Research	Organization	Fluency/ Word Choice	Sources	Deadline
Outstanding 4	Consistent use of conventions/ punctuation. Minor errors do not detract from ideas	Reader interested throughout paper. Writing is original. Expresses personality.	Correct/ interesting information/ details. Research questions answered.	I-Search form used. All five sections labeled. Order is smooth and controlled.	Focused. Ideas related consistently. Varied sentences/ word choices.	Five sources completely recorded.	Turned in on time or before. Complete.
Good 3	Generally shows good use of conventions. Minor errors evident. Does not detract from ideas.	Reader interested through most of paper. Writer generally expresses personality.	Good information and ideas. Two-thirds of research questions answered. Presentation of ideas interesting.	I-Search form used. Four sections labeled. Order is generally smooth.	Mostly focused. Ideas related. Sentences and words have some variation.	Four sources recorded.	Turned in on time. 85 percent complete.
Satisfactory 2	Limited control of conventions weakens overall flow.	Reader sometimes interested in paper. Limited expression of personality.	Satisfactory information and ideas. One-half of questions answered. Ideas forced.	I-Search form partially followed. Three sections labeled. Order somewhat logical.	Somewhat focused. Some confusion. Lacking sentence and word variation.	Three sources recorded.	Turned in on time. 70 percent complete.
Needs Improvement 1	Very little evidence writer uses conventions correctly.	Reader not interested. No sense of personality.	Incomplete information and ideas. One-fourth of questions answered.	I-Search form not followed. Sections not labeled.	Not focused. Sentences confusing.	One or two sources recorded.	Turned in late. 50 percent complete.
Cannot be Scored	Task not attempted.	Task not attempted.	Task not attempted.	Task not attempted.	Task not attempted.	Task not attempted.	Task not attempted.
Student							
Teacher							

Figure 7-2. I-Search Paper Rubric

Communication Rubric							
	Eye Contact	Poise	Volume/ Rate	Visual Aids	Enunciation	Organization	Deadline
Outstanding 4	Presenter makes consistent eye contact with audience.	Presenter uses hands/body appropriately.	Presenter speaks evenly and is not too loud or too soft.	Presenter uses visual aids effectively 90 percent of time.	Presenter speaks very clearly and is easily understood.	Presenter very organized with note cards/visual aids.	Presentation ready before or on morning of due date.
Good 3	Presenter makes eye contact with audience most of time.	Presenter uses hands and body appropriately most of time.	Presenter speaks evenly and at a good volume.	Presenter uses visual aids effectively 80 percent of time.	Presenter speaks clearly.	Presenter organized with note cards and visual aids.	Presentation ready at time of speech.
Satisfactory 2	Presenter makes eye contact with audience some of the time.	Presenter uses hands/body in ways that are distracting some of time.	Presenter speaks at fair volume/rate.	Presenter uses visual aids satisfactorily 70 percent of time.	Presenter speaks clearly some of time.	Presenter somewhat organized and has note cards and visual aids.	Presentation ready at end of day on due date.
Needs Improvement 1	Presenter does not make eye contact with audience.	Presenter uses hands/body inappropriately and are distracting to speech.	Presenter is difficult to understand due to problems in volume/rate.	Presenter uses visual aids ineffectively 50 percent of time.	Presenter does not speak clearly and is difficult to understand.	Presenter disorganized. Presentation hard to follow.	Presentation is one to three days late.
Cannot be Scored	Task not attempted.	Task not attempted.	Task not attempted.	Task not attempted.	Task not attempted.	Task not attempted.	Task not attempted.
Student							
Teacher							

Figure 7-3. Communication Rubric

PowerPoint Rubric						
		Research	Print	Visual Appeal	Citations	Graphics	Writing Conventions
Outstanding 4		Effectively reflects research in I-Search paper.	Print easy to read and enhances the presentation.	Visually pleasing and strengthens message.	Sources properly cited and identified.	Graphics support and enhance topic.	Consistent use of conventions and punctuation.
Good 3		Reflects research in I-Search paper.	Print easy to read but occasionally detracts from presentation.	Most of presentation visually pleasing.	Most sources properly cited and credited.	Topic supported for the most part by graphics	Few mistakes in conventions and punctuation.
Satisfactory 2		Barely reflects research in I-Search paper.	Somewhat illegible.	Some of presentation visually pleasing.	Very few sources properly cited.	Topic vaguely supported by graphics.	Limited control of conventions.
Needs Improvement 1		Does not reflect research.	Difficult to read.	Not visually pleasing.	No citations.	Topic not supported by graphics.	Mistakes distort message.
Cannot be Scored		Task not attempted.	Task not attempted.	Task not attempted.	Task not attempted.	Task not attempted.	Task not attempted.
Student							
Teacher							

Figure 7-4. PowerPoint Rubric

I-Search Journal Portfolio Checklist

_____1. Project Web

_____2. Possible I-Search Topics

_____3. I-Search Topic Homework

_____4. Question Chart

_____5. Product Contract

_____6. I-Search Action Plan

_____7. Wonderful Words

_____8. Keyword Pathfinder

_____9. Interview Form

_____10. Note Sheet

_____11. Search Log

_____12. Resource Finder

_____13. Summary Board—Summary Boxes

_____14. Summary Board—Drawings and Graphs

_____15. Summary Board—Main Idea

_____16. Summary Board—Bibliography

_____17. Summary of the Search

_____18. Completed Summary Board— "Why I chose this topic" and Question Chart

_____19. I-Search Paper, Picture of Product, and Presentation

_____20. Presentation Forms

_____21. Self-Evaluation Forms

_____22. Rubrics—I-Search Paper, Product, Presentation

Figure 7-5. I-Search Journal Portfolio Checklist

SELF-EVALUATION

The self-evaluation is a written paragraph that allows students to assess the process, evaluate what was done well and what could have been done better, and make plans for the future. This, too, is completed at the end of the unit after the celebration and is part of the I-Search Journal Portfolio. See Figure 7-6.

I-SEARCH ACTION PLAN—HOW WILL I KNOW I DID A GOOD JOB?

Wrapping up the unit for the students happens when the class revisits the I-Search Action Plan in the student I-Search Journals. The last question of the planner asks: "How will I know I did a good job?" Review Figure 3-20 with the students and have them make sure they have completed the I-Search paper rubric, I-Search product rubric, I-Search presentation rubric, I-Search Journal Portfolio checklist, and self-evaluation. Work with those students who have not completed the checklist so that their records will be complete.

TEACHER ASSESSMENTS

STANDARDS-BASED GRADE SHEET

There are five questions and 20 lessons in the I-Search Unit. Within these lessons are 23 activities for which students can receive a grade. The lessons/activities are correlated to the McREL Standard/ Benchmarks.

These standards and benchmarks are integrated into the lessons of the I-Search unit and reflect the reading and writing objectives that are commonly tested on the standardized tests. This insures that students are being taught and assessed on material they need to master in order to succeed on those tests. Record their achievement on the standards-based grade sheet. See Figure 7-7.

COLLABORATIVE UNIT ASSESSMENT

The unit evaluation is usually the step that gets skipped in the teaching process. Teachers and the LMS are always short on time. After having spent so many hours planning and teaching a unit of this magnitude, it's easy to just box up the materials and put them aside until it's time to teach it again next year. It's important, though, to take a few

Self-Evaluation

   During my research on_____

I learned how to_____.

I will be able to apply what I learned when I

_____.

The thing I did best was_____.

I can improve _____.

The people who helped me were_____.

They helped me_____.

The thing I liked best about doing this research

was_____.

Figure 7-6. Self-Evaluation

Standards-Based Grade Sheet Example							
Activities	McREL W-1	McREL W-2	McREL Res-4	McREL R-5	McREL R -7	McREL L/S-8	Date	Grade
Big/Little Questions	X		X	X				
Developing Research Questions	X		X	X				
I-Search Action Plan	X		X					
Careful Reader Strategies				X	X			
Wonderful Words	X		X	X	X			
Journal Reflections	X	X	X	X				
Keyword Search	X		X	X	X			
Interview Form	X					X		
Note Sheets	X		X		X			
Search Logs	X		X		X			
Friendly Letter	X			X	X			
Fact/Opinion			X		X			
Summarizing Notes	X		X		X			
Big Book	X		X	X	X			
Summary Boards (summaries in order)	X		X					
Summary illustrations	X		X					
Main Idea	X				X			
Citing Sources	X		X					
Search Summary	X		X					

Figure 7-7. Standards-Based Grade Sheet Example

Activities	McREL W-1	McREL W-2	McREL Res-4	McREL R-5	McREL R -7	McREL L/S-8	Date	Grade
I-Search Paper	X	X	X					
Product						X		
Presentation						X		
I-Search Journal Portfolio	X	X	X	X	X	X		
Average Grade								
McREL W—Writing Standards McREL Res—Research Standards				McREL R—Reading Standards McREL L/S—Listening/Speaking Standards				

Figure 7-7. Standards-Based Grade Sheet Example, continued

minutes to sit down together and review what worked and what needs improvement. A Teacher/Library Media Specialist Evaluation of a Collaboratively Taught Unit from is enclosed to aid in this process. See Figure 7-8.

The I-Search Unit trip ends with the celebration and assessment of the unit as students share the information they've learned, the questions they've answered, the discoveries they've made, and the assessment of the job they've done. Together you've strengthened the community of learners between your students, the LMS, other teachers, parents, and the administration. Congratulations! That's what it takes to help your students succeed academically and in life.

Teacher/Library Media Specialist Evaluation of a Collaboratively Taught Unit (To be completed as a team)

Unit title: _____

Grade Level: _____   # Students Affected: _____

What worked well in the unit?

Suggestions for improvement:

What information skills were integrated into the unit?

From both the teacher's and library media specialist's points of view, did collaboration enhance this unit?

_____Yes   _____No   Why? _____

Was the unit successful enough to warrant doing again in the future?

_____Yes   _____No   Why? _____

How well did the library collection respond to the unit objectives?
Scale: 5=excellent; 4= above average; 3= average; 2= below average; 1= poor

_____   Diversity of formats (paper, audiovisual, electronic)?
_____   Currency (books and other materials up to date)?
_____   Availability (enough materials for the number of students taught)?
_____   Level of students' reading/viewing/listening needs met?
_____   Average of above ratings

What materials/technology will we need if we are planning to repeat the unit again? (Attach list.)

(Source: *Taxonomies of the School Library Media Program*, 2nd ed., by David V. Loertscher. ©1999, Hi Willow Research and Publishing (www.davidvl.org).

Figure 7-8. Teacher/Library Media Specialist Evaluation of a Collaboratively Taught Unit

III CONNECTING I-SEARCH WITH TEACHING TOOLS

TEACHER/TEAM/
LIBRARY MEDIA SPECIALIST
COLLABORATIVE
PLANNING GUIDE

Teacher/Team: LMS:

Unit Topic:

Lessons	Estimated Time	Person/s Responsible
Curriculum correlations, schedule, and planning	Two planning sessions four–six weeks before unit	Teacher/Team and LMS

Establish Timeline (Figure 3-2)
Planning: Teaching: Unit Celebration: Unit Assessments:

Choose the Standards
• Science or Social Studies • Language Arts (Reading, Writing, Listening, Speaking) Standards • Information Literacy Standards • Other Standards (e.g., Technology Standards)

I-Search Unit Concepts

1.

2.

3.

4.

• Construct I-Search Journal

• Determine Unit Assessment

Chapter 3: What Do We Want to Know?

Lesson 1: Unit Introduction—Parts 1, 2, 3, 4	Four to five 30–45-minute sessions	Teacher or LMS

Activities to Unit Introduction:

   • Introductory Activities (Part 1)

   • Student Project Map (Part 2) (Figure 3-8)

   • Skimming and Scanning (Part 3)

   • I-Search Topic Homework (Figures 3-9 and 3-10)

Materials Needed:

Student I-Search Journal (Focus on Figures 3-8, 3-9, and 3-10)

Lesson 2: Develop the Questions—Part 1 and 2	Two to three 30–45-minute sessions	Teacher/LMS

Review unit concepts and help students decide on I-Search questions and project.

Materials Needed: Student I-Search Journal (Focus on Figure 3-12)

Lesson 3: Develop I-Search Action Plan	One 30–45-minute session	Teacher with LMS support

Put I-Search Action Plan on a poster along with product rubrics and place them around the room. Use a completed I-Search Student Journal for an example as well. Product examples: Product rubrics:

Materials Needed: Student I-Search Journal (Focus on Figures 3-14, 3-15, 3-16, 3-17, 3-18, 3-19, 3-20, and 3-21)

Chapter 4: Where Can We Find the Information?

Lesson 4: Establish Careful Reader Strategies	One 30–45-minute session	Teacher and LMS

Choose a high-interest book on the unit topic to teach words in context.

Title:

Author:

Materials Needed:

Student I-Search Journal (Focus on Figure 4-1)

Lesson 5: Incorporate Context Clues and Vocabulary Development	One to two 30–45-minute sessions	Teacher or LMS

Book used in Lesson 4:

Title: Author:

Reference Sources:

Title:

Materials Needed:

Student I-Search Journal (Focus on Figures 4-2, 4-3)

Lesson 6: Design Keyword Searches	One 30–45-minute session	Teacher or LMS

Research Resources:

CD-ROM:

Encyclopedia Index (print):

Encyclopedia (online):

Information Books/Special Encyclopedia:

Materials Needed:

Student I-Search Journal (Focus on Figure 4-4)

Lesson 7: Develop Meaning with Reciprocal Teaching	One 45-minute session	Teacher or LMS

Materials Needed:

Student I-Search Journal (Focus on Figure 4-5)

Lesson 8: Interview Experts	One 30–45-minute session	Teacher or LMS

Brainstorm to come up with possible experts for the unit. Star the best ones.

Materials Needed:

Student I-Search Journal (Focus on Figures 4-6 and 4-7)

Chapter 5: How Will We Understand and Record the Information We Find?

Lesson 9: Take Notes and Cite Sources	One 45–60-minute session	Teacher or LMS

- Picture or poster related to unit to teach detail (who, what, when, where, and why)

- Two articles that will answer unit questions from an information book or online source with headings, subheadings, bolded test, graphs, captions, and pictures

Materials Needed:

Student I-Search Journal (Focus on Figures 5-1 and 5-5)

Lesson 10: Differentiate Between Fact and Opinion	One 30–45-minute session	Teacher or LMS

Find a high-interest book or video/DVD that illustrates fact and opinion and addresses a unit concept.

Additional materials:

Lesson 11: Evaluation of Web Site Authenticity	One 30–45-minute session	LMS or Teacher

Web sites to be used for evaluation lesson:

Additional materials:

Lesson 12: Develop Research Skills Workshop	Three to five 45–60-minute sessions	LMS and Teacher

Work together to determine information skills needed to do research in the LMC. The LMS will develop and teach the important skill lessons and locate needed resources and materials. Make decisions in regard to research opportunities (e.g., groups, centers, independent research). Provide sufficient time for students to research and take notes.

Skill lessons:

Research opportunities:

LMS developed "Resource Finder" (See Figure 5-9)

- Reference books

- Nonfiction/information books

- Internet sites

- Online encyclopedias

- Other online resources

Materials Needed:

Student I-Search Journal (See Figures 3-18, 4-3, 4-4, 5-1, 5-5, and 5-9)

Lesson 13: Summarize Notes	One to two 30–45-minute sessions	Teacher or LMS

Students will need to be finished taking notes and have their Note Sheets ready to summarize. Teacher will need examples of Note Sheets in order to demonstrate the summarization process.

Materials Needed:

Student I-Search Journal—Note Sheets from research

Chapter 6: How Will We Show What We Learned?

Lesson 14: Construct Summary Boards	One 30–45-minute session	Teacher or LMS

Choose a picture or information book previously used in the unit that lends itself to a sequencing activity.

Title:

Author:

Create a Summary Board for each student or help students construct their own boards. Have teacher Note Sheets available to show students how the summary boxes go together.

Materials Needed:

Student I-Search Journal (Focus on Figures 6-1 and 6-2)

Lesson 15: Draw Conclusions	One 45–60-minute session	Teacher or LMS

Find a thought-provoking picture/poster on the unit to teach drawing conclusions. Picture source: Page #/Web address:

Design example of drawings and graphs on the Summary Board example to share with students. See Figure 6-4.

Materials Needed: Student I-Search Journal (Focus on Figure 6-4)

Lesson 16: Develop Main Idea	One 45–60-minute session	Teacher or LMS

Find a book or story that will address a unit concept and clearly show how facts support the main idea. Title: Author:

Develop a graphic that illustrates the main idea of the unit. See Figure 6-5.

Materials Needed: Student I-Search Journal (Focus on Figures 6-5 and 6-6)

Lesson 17: List Sources	One 30–45-minute session	Teacher or LMS

Create a teacher example with sources cut apart, arranged in alphabetical order and glued on the Summary Boards.

Materials Needed:

Student I-Search Journal (Focus on Figure 6-7)

Lesson 18: Summarize the Search	One to two 30–45-minute sessions	Teacher with LMS support

Develop an example of a Search Summary using a completed Search Log. Be ready to glue it on the Summary Board.

Materials Needed:

Student I-Search Journal (Focus on Figures 6-9 and 6-11)

Lesson 19: Organize Writing Workshop	Two to three 45–60-minute sessions	Teacher with LRS

Using the five steps of the writing process (see Figure 6-12) and incorporating the six writing traits, develop an example of a completed I-Search paper or use outstanding student papers from previous units.

Materials Needed:

Student I-Search Journal (Focus on Figures 6-12 and 6-13)

Lesson 20: Produce Products, Presentations, and Create Celebrations	Four to five 45–60-minute sessions	Teacher or LMS

- Students should make a final decision on the product they will produce to show what they have learned. See Figure 6-14.

- Create rubrics and present to students before they begin making their products. See Chapter 7.

- Determine Presentation/Listening Lessons

Materials Needed:

Student I-Search Journal (Focus on Figure 6-16)

Lesson 20 (Continued)		

Decide how students will present and display their products as part of the Unit Celebration.

Unit Celebration:

Student Presentation:

Product Display:

Materials Needed:

Student I-Search Journal (Focus on Figure 6-16)

Chapter 7: How Will We Know We Did a Good Job?

Assessment	Ongoing and one day at end of unit	Teacher and LMS

Refer to Chapter 7 for assessment procedures. This step should be done prior to teaching the unit in order to start with the assessment in mind. Assessments include:

- I-Search paper rubric (Figure 7-2)
- PowerPoint Rubric (Figure 7-4)
- Communication Rubric (Figure 7-3)
- I-Search Journal Portfolio Checklist (Figure 7-5)
- Standards-Based Grade Sheet (Figure 7-7)
- Student Self-evaluation (Figure 7-6)
- I-Search Action Planner (Figures 3-16, 3-18, 3-19, 3-20, and 3-21)
- Teacher/Library Media Specialist Evaluation of a Collaboratively Taught Unit (Figure 7-8)

Record below the assessments that will be used:

Materials Needed:

Student I-Search Journal (Focus on Figures 7-5, 7-6, and 3-21 plus rubrics)

Additional Activities

Description of Activity	Where does this activity need to be added?	Materials Needed	Person Responsible

Unit Resources

I-Search Journal

Name _____

Topic _____

Date _____

I-SEARCH ACTION

QUESTION   **When I develop questions**

EXPLORE   **When I find information**

CREATE   **When I use the information I find**

PRESENT   **When I share my information and ideas**

JUDGE   **When I decide if I did my best**

©Roger von Oech. 1986. From *A Kick in the Seat of the Pants*. For more information go to http://creativethink.com.

Figure 3-14. I-Search Action

Question

⬇

When I develop questions

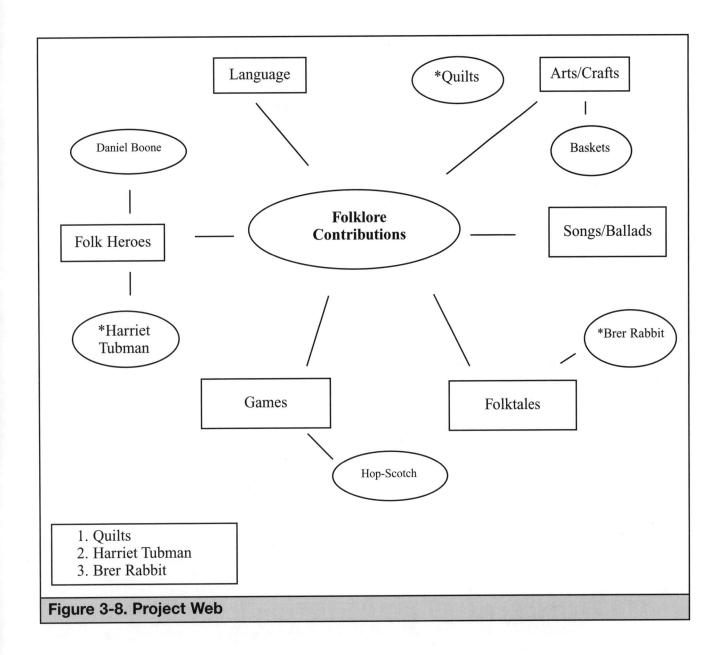

Figure 3-8. Project Web

Possible I-Search Topics

My first choice of a topic is _____

because _____

_____ .

My second choice of a topic is _____

because _____

_____ .

My third choice of a topic is _____

because _____

_____ .

Figure 3-9. Possible I-Search Topics

I-Search Topic Homework

1. **Take your first three topic choices home to share with your family.**

2. **Discuss your family's ideas and suggestions.**

3. **Make a decision based on your interests and whether there is enough information available to write a good research paper and product.**

4. **Return this homework to your teacher to be added to your I-Search Journal.**

I-Search Topic _____

Student _____

Parent _____

Date _____

Figure 3-10. I-Search Topic Homework

What do I know?	What do I want to find out?	What are my research questions?

"Pre-Notetaking Sheet" source: Joyce, Marilyn L. and Julie I. Tallman. 1997. *Making the Writing and Research Connection with the I-Search Process: A How-to-Do-It Manual for Teachers and School Librarians.* Reprinted with permission from the Publisher. Copyright © 1997 by Neal-Schuman Publishers, Inc.

Figure 3-12. Question Chart

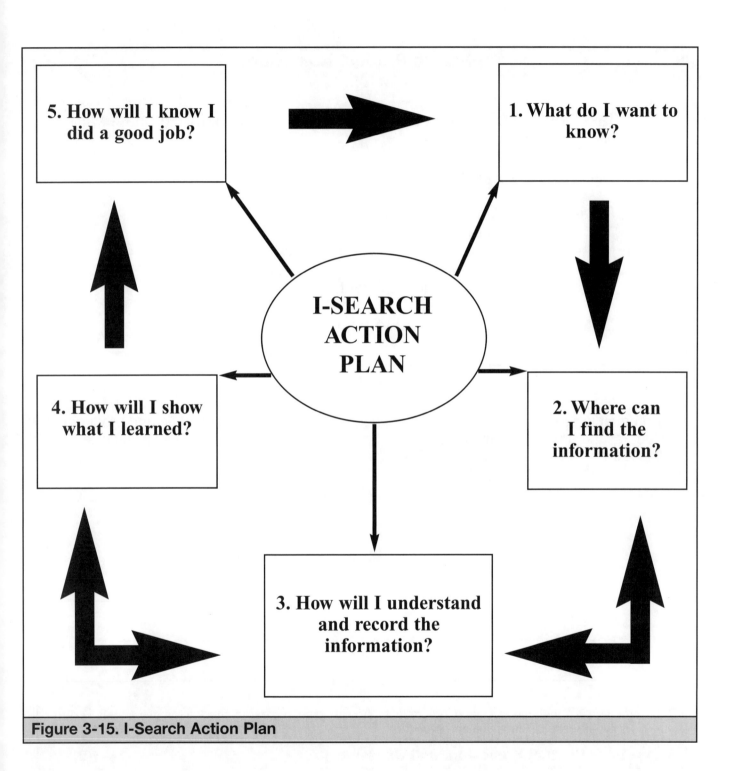

Figure 3-15. I-Search Action Plan

I-Search Product Homework

1. Take your list of product choices and the rubrics home to share with your family.

2. Discuss the suggestions with them.

3. Review the rubric for your product.

4. Make a decision about the product you want to make.

5. Sign the attached product contract.

6. Return the product contract to your teacher.

Product Contract

My product is going to be a _____ . My presentation and product will include all the answers to my questions and any additional information I feel is important. I will follow the specific guidelines found on the rubric for my product.

I will have my product ready at the beginning of class on _____ .

Student _____

Parent _____

Teacher _____

Date _____

Please return this sheet. You may keep the product rubric at home in order to check the requirements while working on your product. Thank you and have fun!

Figure 3-16. Product Homework and Contract

What Do I Want to Know?

1. _____

2. _____

3. _____

4. _____

5. _____

Figure 3-17. What Do I Want to Know?

Where Can I Find the Information?

1. _____

2. _____

3. _____

4. _____

5. _____

Figure 3-18. Where Can I Find the Information?

How Will I Understand and Record the Information I Find?

- _____Note Sheets

- _____Search Log

- _____Resource Finder

- _____Main Idea Graphic

- _____Summary Board

- _____Summary of the Search

Figure 3-19. How Will I Understand and Record the Information I Find?

How Will I Show What I Learned?

- Date due: _____ I-Search Paper _____

- Date due: _____ Product _____

- Date due: _____ Presentation _____

- Date due: _____ I-Search Journal Portfolio _____

Figure 3-20. How Will I Show What I Learned?

How Will I Know I Did a Good Job?

_____I-Search paper rubric completed

_____I-Search product rubric completed

_____I-Search presentation rubric completed

_____I-Search Journal Portfolio completed

_____Self-evaluation completed

Figure 3-21. How Will I Know I Did a Good Job?

Explore

↓

When I find information

What a Careful Reader Does

Before reading, a careful reader asks:

- **Why am I reading this story or article?**

- **What does this seem to be about?**
    Is it about something or someone I already know?
    Is it about something new I am learning?
    Is it about something I want to learn?

- **What kind of reading will I do?**
    Will I read about characters in a story?
    Will I read about how to do something?
    Will I read to learn interesting facts?

During reading, a careful reader asks:

- **Do I understand what I'm reading?**
    Can I figure out any words I don't know?
    Do I need to slow down?
    Do I need to look for clues?
    Do I need to read some parts again?

- **How can I connect with what I'm reading?**
    Is it something I already know?
    Is it something new I am learning?
    Is it something I want to know more about?

After reading, a careful reader asks:

- **What do I remember about what I read?**
    Can I use my own words to tell others about it?
    Can I name the most important ideas in it?
    Can I think of other ways to show that I understand it?

- **What do I think about what I read?**
    Did it add to something I already knew?
    Did it tell me something new?
    Did it make me want to learn more?

Source: Texas Education Agency. 2003. *Grade 3: TAKS Study Guide*. Austin: TX. Copyright © 2003. Texas Education Agency.

Figure 4-1. What a Careful Reader Does

CONTEXT CLUES

Synonym—A word that means the same or almost the same thing as another word (big and large).

*It takes a long time to **construct** a bridge. Workers took several years to **build** the Golden Gate Bridge.*

Antonym—A word that means the opposite of another word (hot and cold).

*The lion looked **tame** but it was **wild**.*

Explanations, Definitions, and Descriptions—A group of words that define, explain, or describe the meaning of another word.

*Todd was in the **choir** at his old school. He hopes his new school will also have a **group that sings songs together**.*

Example—An example is an item that belongs in a group because it is like other things in the group.

*Tran wants to be an **author** when he grows up. He wants to write like his favorite author, **Dr. Seuss**.*

Source: Texas Education Agency. 2003. *Grade 3: TAKS Study Guide*. Austin: TX. Copyright © 2003. Texas Education Agency.

Figure 4-2. Context Clues

Wonderful Words

WORD	GUESS THE MEANING	DICTIONARY DEFINITION	PICTURE OF DEFINITION

Figure 4-3. Wonderful Words

Keyword	Source
	Title_____ Author/Publisher_____ Call Number/Web site_____
	Title_____ Author/Publisher_____ Call Number/Web site_____
	Title_____ Author/Publisher_____ Call Number/Web site_____
	Title_____ Author/Publisher_____ Call Number/Web site_____
	Title_____ Author/Publisher_____ Call Number/Web site_____

Figure 4-4. Keyword Pathfinder

RECIPROCAL TEACHING

Summarizing

Questioning

Clarifying

Predicting

Figure 4-5. Reciprocal Teaching

Interview Etiquette

1. Experts and authorities are helpful sources of information when you are doing research. These people are those who know a lot about something. They do not need to hold an official position.

2. Contact the person with a letter, phone call, fax, and/or e-mail before interviewing them. Decide which way is the best approach for your situation.

3. Take careful notes. If a tape recorder is used, be sure to ask permission to use it.

4. Your questions need to be prepared ahead of time. However, ask additional questions if you see a good opportunity.

5. Ask your experts where they go to find more information and answers.

6. Be sure to ask questions that require more than just a "yes" or "no" answer (ask "Big questions").

7. Close the interview with a thank you. Let them know that you appreciate their time. You may also want to send a thank-you note.

Figure 4-6. Interview Etiquette

Interview Form

Name of person interviewed_____

Title of person interviewed_____

Date of interview_____

Person conducting interview_____

    1.   Question:

           Answer:

    2.   Question:

           Answer:

    3.   Question:

           Answer:

    4.   Question:

           Answer:

Put the completed interview form in your I-Search Journal after showing it to your teacher.

Figure 4-7. Interview Form

Create

↓

When I use the information I find

Note Sheet

Name _____**Topic:**_____

Question:

Notes:	Source:
p.	
Notes:	Source:
p.	

Summary:

Figure 5-1. Note Sheet

Search Log

Date _____

What have I done so far? _____

How have I done? _____

What do I need to do next? _____

Date: _____

What have I done so far? _____

How have I done? _____

What do I need to do next? _____

Date _____

What have I done so far? _____

How have I done? _____

What do I need to do next? _____

Figure 5-5. Search Log

Resource Finder

Reference Books:	Non-fiction/Information Books:
1.	1.
2	2
3.	3.
4.	4.
Online Reference Sources:	**Online Periodicals:**
1.	1.
2	2
3.	3.
4.	4.
Web Sites:	**Web Sites:**
1.	1.
2	2
3.	3.
4.	4.

Figure 5-9. Resource Finder

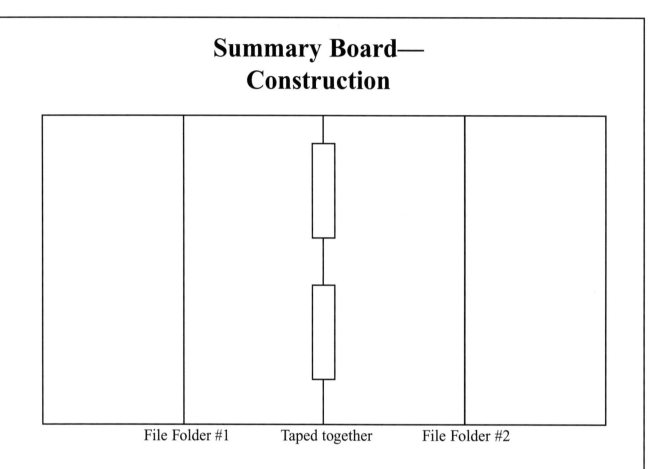

Summary Board—
Construction

File Folder #1   Taped together   File Folder #2

Directions:

- Construct a Summary Board.

- Tape two file folders together.

- Put your name in the upper right-hand corner.

- Place it in your I-Search Journal.

Figure 6-1. Summary Board—Construction

Summary Board— Summary Boxes

1		4	
2		5	
3		6	
Summary Boxes		Summary Boxes	

Directions:

- Cut summary boxes off Note Sheets.

- Arrange them in logical order that tells a story.

- Glue them on the Summary Board.

Figure 6-2. Summary Board—Summary Boxes

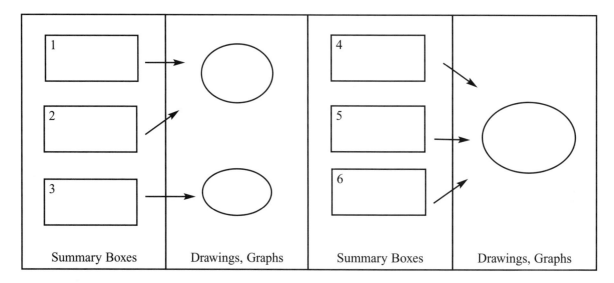

Summary Board— Drawing and Graphs

Directions:

- Illustrate summaries with drawings, charts, and graphs.

- Some drawings may apply to more than one summary.

Figure 6-4. Summary Board—Drawing and Graphs

Main Idea Flag Graphic

Figure 6-5. Main Idea Flag Graphic

Summary Board—
Main Idea

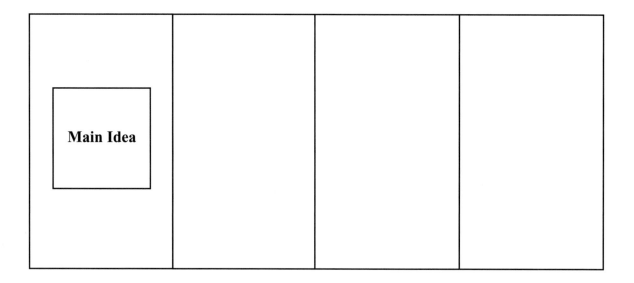

Back of Summary Board

Directions:

- Compelte Main Idea graphic. See Figure 6-5.

- Give the graphic on the left-hand side of the back of the Summary Board.

- See illustration above.

Figure 6-6. Summary Board—Main Idea

Summary Board—Bibliography

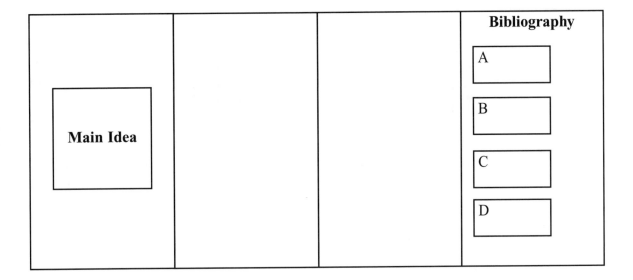

Bibliography

A

B

C

D

Main Idea

Directions:

- Cut bibliography information from Note Sheets.

- Arrange them in alphabetical order according to the author.

- Glue them on the Summary Board.

Figure 6-7. Summary Board—Bibliography

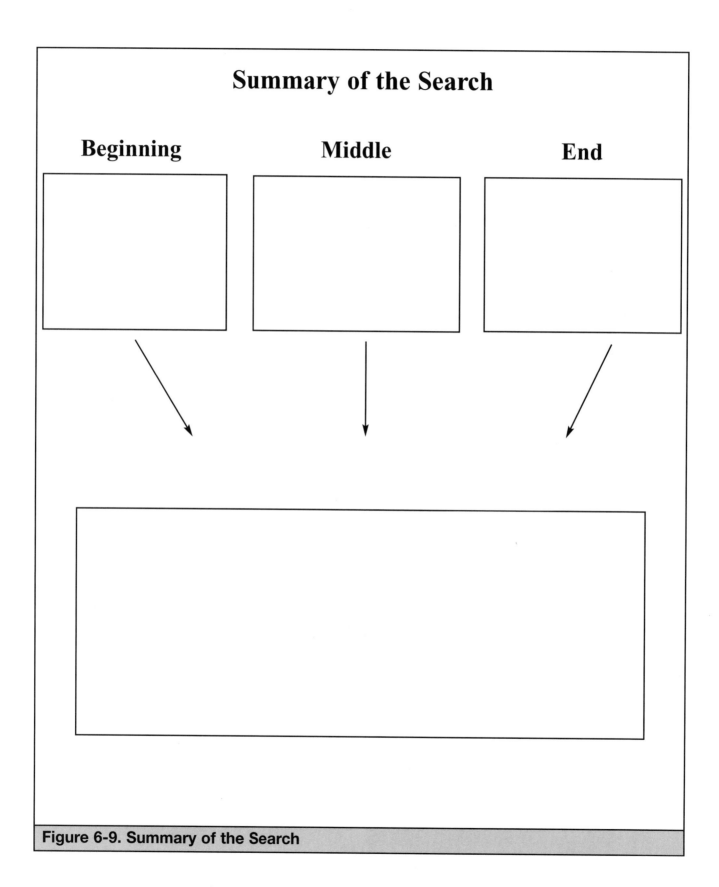

Figure 6-9. Summary of the Search

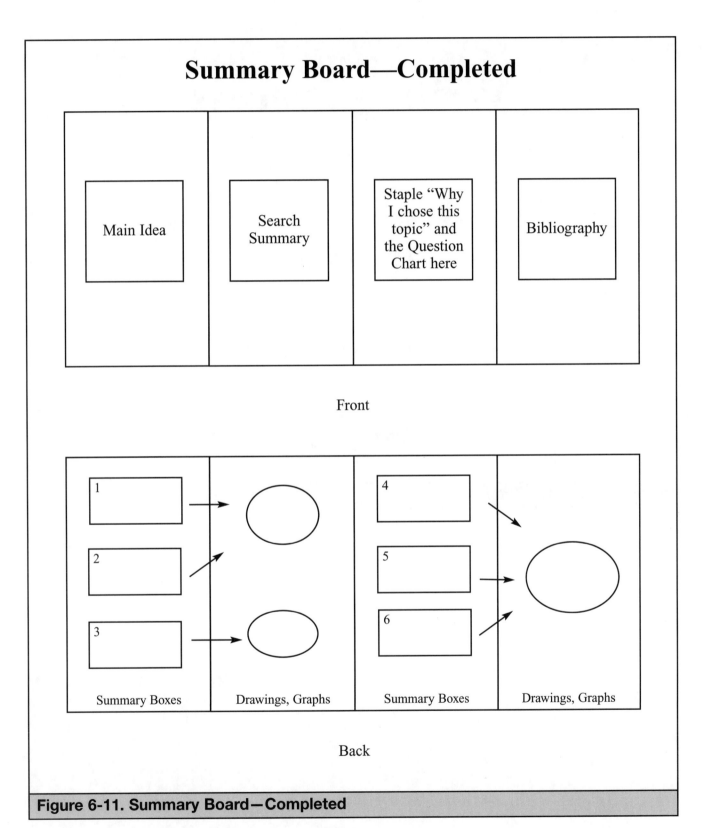

Figure 6-11. Summary Board—Completed

Writing Process

Prewriting

Drafting

Revising and editing

Final copy

Figure 6-12. Writing Process

Revising and Editing

(-) Put one line through things you want to take out.

(^) Use a caret to add letters, words, and/or sentences.

◯   Circle words that are misspelled.

(≡) Put three lines under letters that need to be capitalized.

(.) (?) (!) Add any punctuation that is missing.

(/) Put a slash through any letters that need to be lower case.

Figure 6-13. Revising and Editing

Present

↓

When I share my information and ideas

Staple I-Search Paper here with picture of product and presentation.

Presenter _____ **Topic**_____

What I learned:

_____

Presenter _____ **Topic**_____

What I learned:

_____

Presenter _____ **Topic**_____

What I learned:

Figure 6-15. Presentations

Judge

↓

When I decide if I did my best

Staple Rubrics Here

- Research Paper Rubric

- Product Rubric

- Presentation Rubric

I-Search Journal Portfolio Checklist

_____ 1. Project Web

_____ 2. Possible I-Search Topics

_____ 3. I-Search Topic Homework

_____ 4. Question Chart

_____ 5. Product Contract

_____ 6. I-Search Action Plan

_____ 7. Wonderful Words

_____ 8. Keyword Pathfinder

_____ 9. Interview Form

_____ 10. Note Sheet

_____ 11. Search Log

_____ 12. Resource Finder

_____ 13. Summary Board—Summary Boxes

_____ 14. Summary Board—Drawings and Graphs

_____ 15. Summary Board—Main Idea

_____ 16. Summary Board—Bibliography

_____ 17. Summary of the Search

_____ 18. Completed Summary Board— "Why I chose this topic" and Question Chart

_____ 19. I-Search Paper, Picture of Product, and Presentation

_____ 20. Presentation Forms

_____ 21. Self-Evaluation Forms

_____ 22. Rubrics—I-Search Paper, Product, Presentation

Figure 7-5. I-Search Journal Portfolio Checklist

Self-Evaluation

During my research on_____

I learned how to_____.

I will be able to apply what I learned when I

_____.

The thing I did best was_____.

I can improve _____.

The people who helped me were_____.

They helped me_____.

The thing I liked best about doing this research

was_____.

Figure 7-6. Self-Evaluation

MODEL I-SEARCH UNIT: OUR NATIONAL HERITAGE—THIS LAND IS OUR LAND

Teacher/Team: Librarian:

Unit Topic: National Heritage—This Land Is Our Land

Lessons	Estimated Time	Person/s Responsible
Curriculum correlations, schedule, and planning	Two planning sessions 4–6 weeks before unit	Teacher/Team and LMS

Standards/objectives addressed in unit:

- Content standards: McREL History Standard 6: Understand the folklore and other cultural contributions from various regions of the United States and how they helped form a national heritage (See Figure 3-5)

- Language Arts Standards: McREL Language Arts Standards (See Lessons 1–20)

- Information Literacy Standards (See Lessons 1–20)

Unit Timeline

Planning:

Teaching:

Unit Celebration:

Unit Assessments:

I-Search Unit Concepts

1. The United States is divided into four regions (Northeast, South, Midwest, and West)
2. People are different in each of the four regions.
3. Cultural contributions such as legends, ballads, games, arts, crafts, music, and language describe the environment, lifestyles, beliefs, and struggles of people in the four regions both today and long ago.
4. All regions have folk heroes who have contributed to the cultural history of the United States.
5. Cultural contributions from all regions combine to form the National Heritage.

• Construct I-Search Journal—Part III-B
• Determine Unit Assessments—Chapter 7

Chapter 3: What Do We Want to Know?

Lesson 1: Unit Introduction	Four to five 30–45-minute sessions	Teacher with LMS

Activities to Unit Introduction:

See Chapter 3—Lesson 1: Unit Introduction

Materials Needed:
   • *People* by Peter Spier (book and video)
   • *This Land Is Your Land* by Woody Guthrie (book and video)
   • Wall-size U.S. map displayed
   • Variety of quilts plus videos, pictures, slides
   • Chart paper, poster boards, transparencies
   • Markers, pens
   • I-Search Journal for each student (Figures 3-8, 3-9, and 3-10)
   • Access to LMC

Lesson 2: Develop the Questions—Parts 1 and 2	Two to three 30–45-minute sessions	Teacher and LMS

Review unit concepts and help students develop I-Search questions and decide on I-Search project. Record required questions below.

Unit Concepts (Figure 3-7) – Project Web (Figure 3-8)

Nonnegotiable student questions:

1. Which region and folklore contribution in that region do I want to learn about?
2. How does that contribution describe the environment, lifestyles, beliefs, and struggles of the people in that region?

Materials Needed:

Lesson 2: Parts 1 and 2—Develop Big and Little Questions and Develop Research Questions

- Big and Little questions T-Chart on poster, transparency, or chart paper
- KWL Chart on poster, chart paper, or transparency
- Colored markers or transparency pens
- Student I-Search Journals (Focus on Figure 3-12)

Lesson 3: Develop I-Search Action Plan	One 30–45 minute session	Teacher with LMS support

Put I-Search Action Plan on a poster along with product rubrics and place them around the room. A completed I-Search Student Journal is also needed as an example.

Product examples: Figure 6-14

Product rubrics: Chapter 7 (Figures 7-2, 7-3, and 7-4)

Materials Needed:

- I-Search Action (Figure 3-14) and I-Search Action Plan (Figure 3-15) on charts
- Wall calendar
- I-Search Journals (Focus on Figures 3-14, 3-15, 3-16, 3-17, 3-18, 3-19, 3-20, and 3-21)
- Transparency of Note Sheet (Figure 5-1)

Chapter 4: Where Can We Find the Information?

Lesson 4: Establish Careful Reader Strategies	One 30–45-minute session	Teacher or LMS

Decide on a high-interest book on the unit topic to teach words in context.

Title: *Abuela*, by Arthur Dorros

Materials Needed:

- *Abuela*, by Arthur Dorros
- What a Careful Reader Does chart/poster (Figure 4-1)
- Transparency of key pages of book where students will find answers to prepared questions or several copies of the book (with copyright permission secured where needed)
- Sticky notes
- Student I-Search Journal (Focus on Figure 4-1)

Lesson 5: Incorporate Context Clues and Vocabulary Development	One to two 30–45-minute sessions	Teacher or LMS

Book used in Lesson 4: *Abuela*, by Arthur Dorros

Textbook: *Explore Texas,* chapter Two: "Regions of Texas," pages 32–35

Materials Needed:

- Transparency, chart, or poster of Context Clues (Figure 4-2)
- Transparency, chart, or poster of Wonderful Words chart (Figure 4-3)
- Student I-Search Journals (Focus on Figures 4-2 and 4-3)

Lesson 6: Keyword Searches	One 30–45-minute session	Teacher or LMS

Research Resources:

Reference Books: General encyclopedias, atlases, biographical dictionaries, textbooks

Online Reference Sources: Online encyclopedias, atlases, dictionaries, periodical databases

Materials Needed:

Unit concepts on poster, chart, transparency

Student questions in I-Search Journals/I-Search Action Planner (Focus on Figure 4-4)

Library workstations

Lesson 7: Develop Meaning with Reciprocal Teaching	One 30–45-minute session	Teacher or LMS

Use an article from a textbook, reference book, or online resource that addresses a unit concept. The online *Britannica Encyclopedia* article, "Jackie Robinson," is a good example for this unit. It can be accessed at *www.britannica.com*. Search for "Jackie Robinson."

Materials Needed:

- Above article
- Reciprocal Teaching chart (See Figure 4-5)
- Blank paper or letter template on computers for each student
- I-Search Journals (Focus on Figure 4-5)

Lesson 8: Interview Experts	One 30–45-minute session	Teacher or LMS

Brainstorm possible experts in relation to the unit. Star the best ones.

- Storytellers
- Local history experts
- Folk artists (quilters, basket or pottery makers, etc.)
- Folk singers/dancers

Materials Needed:

- Overhead projector
- Transparency of Interview Form (Figure 4-7)
- Blank transparencies/transparency pens
- Transparency of Interview Form (Figure 4-8)
- I-Search Journals (Focus on Figures 4-6 and 4-7)
- Chart and markers
- Story of person's life (magazine, short biography, picture book)
- Expert on unit topic
- Parent permission letter

Chapter 5: How Will We Understand and Record the Information We Find?

Lesson 9: Take Notes and Cite Sources	One 30–45-minute session	Teacher or LMS

- Picture or poster related to unit to teach detail (who, what, when, where, and why)
- Two articles that will address unit concepts from an information book or online source with headings, sub-headings, bolded test, graphs, captions, and pictures.

Materials Needed:
- Internet pictures: Geo-Images Project (http://geoimages.berkeley.edu/GeoImages .html); Smithsonian American Art Museum (http://americanart.si.edu/index2.cfm); Library of Congress, America's Story from America's Library, "Come Celebrate" (www.americaslibrary.gov/cgi-bin/page.cgi/jp/celebrate)
- County and State Fairs (www.americaslibrary.gov/cgi-bin/page.cgi/jp/celebrte/fair_1);
"Rambling Round: The Life and Times of Woody Guthrie" (http://memory.loc.gov/ ammem/wwghtml/wwgessay.html)
- Blank transparency and markers; blank sheets of paper; transparency or computer-generated picture and article; copy of separate article for each student; Note Sheets, Search Log; transparency of Note Sheet
- Student I-Search Journal for each student (Focus on Figures 5-1 and 5-5)

Lesson 10: Differentiate Between Fact and Opinion	One 30–45-minute session	Teacher or LMS

High-interest book, video or DVD that illustrates fact and opinion and answers a unit question

Title: *A Picture Book of Sojourner Truth*, by David A. Adler

Web site: www.sojournertruth.org and www.nationalgeographic.com

Materials Needed:
- Above book
- Fact and Opinion graphic organizer on chart or poster (Figure 5-6)
- Fact and Opinion graphic organizer on charts for groups of two or three students
- Fact and Opinion cards based on the book made by teacher or librarian

Lesson 11: Evaluate Web Site Authenticity	One 30–45-minute session	LMS or Teacher

Internet search activities (Figure 5-8)

Teach online searching with
- www.learnwebskills.com/search/main.html
- www.noodletools.com/debbie/literacies/information/5locate/adviceengine.html

Search engines for students
- www.ala.org/greatsites
- www.ajkids.com/
- www.awesomelibrary.org/
- sunsite.berkeley.edu/KidsClick!/
- www.tekmom.com/search/
- www.yaholligans.com/

Materials Needed:

- Computers with Internet access for each student
- I-Search Journals (Focus on Figure 5-9)

Lesson 12: Develop Research Workshop Skills	Three to five 45–60-minute sessions	LMS and Teacher

Library/Research Skills

Copyright and Plagiarism Lessons

- www.yaholligans.com/tg/citation.html

- http://questioning.org

Research Opportunities

Students will do independent research in order to find the answers to their questions. They will rotate among centers composed of

- Computers that have been bookmarked for folklore and online reference sites
- Library tables with information books on culture and folklore
- Centers near the reference area with access to general and special encyclopedias, atlases, biographical dictionaries, etc.
- Computer stations with CD-ROMs that focus on folklore and cultural contributions
- Video centers with cultural/folklore videos available

Resource Finder developed by LMS (Figure 5-9)

- Reference books
- Nonfiction/Information books
- Internet sites
- Online encyclopedias
- Other on-line resources
- Student I-Search Journal (Focus on Figures 3-17, 4-3, 4-4, 5-1, 5-5, and 5-9)

Note: See Lesson 6 (Design Key Word Searches) for list of reference materials and the Resource List for this unit for additional books and Web sites.

Lesson 13: Summarize Notes	One to two 30–45-minute session	Teacher or LMS

Students will need to have finished taking notes and to have their Note Sheets ready to summarize. Teacher will need examples of Note Sheets in order to demonstrate the summarization process.

Materials Needed:

- Completed Note Sheets and I-Search Journals
- Previously developed Note Sheet on transparency, poster, or chart (See Figure 5-2)
- Previously developed Note Sheet with summary on transparency, poster, or chart (See Figure 5-10)
- Overhead projector and transparency pens or charts/posters and markers

Chapter 6: How Will We Show What We Learned?

Lesson 14: Construct Summary Boards	One 30–45-minute session	Teacher with LMS support

Choose a picture or information book that lends itself to a sequencing activity.

Title: *Goin' Someplace Special,* by Patricia McKissack

Create a summary board for each student or help students construct their own boards. Have teacher's prepared Note Sheets available to show students how the summary boxes go together.

Materials Needed:

- Above picture or information book
- Chart paper or poster board
- Colored markers or map pencils
- Two file folders for each student
- Tape for file folders
- Glue sticks and student scissors
- I-Search Journals (Focus on Figures 6-1 and 6-2)

Lesson 15: Draw Conclusions	One 45–60-minute session	Teacher or LMS

Find a thought-provoking picture or poster on the unit to teach students how to draw conclusions.
- Web site based on the book *On the Trail of the Immigrant*, by Edward A. Stiner (www.digitalhistory.uh.edu/photo_album/photo_album.html)
- *Immigrant Kids* by Russell Freedman

Design example of pictures, charts, and graphs on the Summary Board example to share with students. (See Figure 6-4.)

Materials Needed:
- Transparencies for "Tracks" pictures (See Figure 6-3.)
- Teacher Summary Board with illustrated summaries
- Summary Board for each student
- Markers and map pencils

Lesson 16: Develop Main Idea	One 45–60-minute session	Teacher or LMS

Find a book or story that will answer a question in the unit and clearly show how facts support the main idea.

Title: *The Best Town in the World* (poem in book form), by Byrd Baylor.

Develop a graphic that illustrates the main idea of the unit. (See Figure 6-5.)

Materials Needed:
- Main idea graphic (see above)
- Summary Boards for each student
- Teacher example of Summary Board

| Lesson 17: List Sources | One 30–45-minute session | Teacher or LMS |

Create a teacher example with sources cut apart, arranged in alphabetical order, and glued on the Summary Boards.

Materials Needed:

- I-Search Journals (Focus on Figure 6-7)

- Bibliographic information from Note Sheets

- Glue sticks

- Student scissors

- Student Summary Boards

- Teacher example of completed Summary Boards/Note Sheets with bibliographic information (See Figure 6-7)

| Lesson 18: Summarize the Search | One to two 30–45-minute session | Teacher with LMS support |

Develop an example of a Search Summary using a completed Search Log. Be ready to glue it on the Summary Board.

Materials Needed:

- Student Search Logs in I-Search Journals

- Summary of the Search graphic for each student (See Figure 6-9)

- Transparency for Summary of the Search graphic

- Student and teacher Summary Boards

- Teacher example of completed Search Log and Search Summary graphic (See Figures 6-8 and 6-10)

- Student I-Search Journal (See Figures 6-9 and 6-11)

| Lesson 19: Organize Writing Workshop | Two to three 45–60-minutesessions | Teacher with LMS support |

Using the five steps of the writing process (see Figure 6-12) and incorporating the six writing traits (Writing Workshop) develop an example of a completed I-Search paper or use outstanding student papers from previous units.

Materials Needed:

- Summary Boards for each student
- Blank note-book paper/pencils
- Student I-Search journals (Figures 6-12 and 6-13)
- Poster of Writing Process (Figure 6-12) and Editing and Revising (Figure 6-13)
- Large index cards

| Lesson 20: Produce Products, Make Presentations, and Create Celebrations | Four to five 45–60-minute sessions | Teacher and LRS |

- Students should make a final decision on the product they will produce to show what they have learned. (See Figure 6-14)
- Create rubrics and present to students before they begin making their products. See Chapter 7.

Materials Needed:

- Books:

  Younger students—*Arthur Meets the President,* Marc Brown

  Older students—*Ruby Mae Has Something to Say,* David Small

- Suggested folklore products: model cabin or sod house, regional travel brochure, family survey on place of origins, medicinal herb handbook, folk dance/song/ballad, rodeo diorama, folk story/puppet show, play, quilt, basket, or pottery.
- List of products posted with examples where possible

Lesson 20 (continued)		

Decide how students will present and display their products as part of the Unit Celebration.

Unit Celebration

Folk Festival with music, posters, maps as background for student presentations. Allow 2–3 days for student presentations. Invite parents. Have them sign up for specific days and times so that there is an audience for all of the presentations.

Student Presentations

Students should be prepared for their presentations with presentation lessons that occurred while they were working on their projects at home. They should have their I-Search paper and product for their presentation as well as notes for their speeches.

Product Display

Take a picture of each student with his or her project and glue it to the cover of the I-Search paper for the display so that people will be able to put a picture with a name. Display the products and papers in the LMC or other secure place where parents, teachers, administrators, and students can view them.

Materials Needed:

- Maps, posters, decorations for the Folk Festival

- Overhead projector available for student products

- Camera and film for pictures of each student

- Display space for projects after presentation

- Folk tapes or CDs and tape recorder or CD player

- Student I-Search Journal (Focus on Figure 6-16)

Chapter 7: How Will We Know We Did a Good Job?		
Assessment	Ongoing and one day at end of unit	Teacher and LMS

Refer to Chapter 7 for assessment procedures prior to teaching the unit in order to start with the assessment in mind. Assessments include:

- I-Search Paper Rubric (See Figure 7-2)
- PowerPoint Product Rubric (See Figure 7-4)
- Presentation Rubric (See Figure 7-3)
- I-Search Journal Portfolio Checklist (See Figure 7-5)
- Standards-Based Grade Sheet Example (See Figure 7-7)
- Student Self-Evaluation (See Figure 7-6)
- Teacher/Library Media Specialist Evaluation of Collaboratively Taught Unit (See Figure 7-8)

Possible Assessments:

- All of the above.
- Special rubrics for products such as models, posters, dioramas, songs, dance, puppet shows/plays, and craft projects such as quilts, baskets, and pottery.
- Additional product rubrics, as found at the RubricBuilder site (www.landmark-project.com/classweb/tools/rubric_builder.php) and Rubistar (http://rubistar.4teachers.org/index.php).

Materials Needed:

- Copies of rubrics displayed around the room
- Example of a student I-Search Journal Portfolio
- Examples or pictures of products
- Copies of Standards-Based Grade Sheet
- Copies of Teacher/Librarian Evaluation of Collaboratively Taught Unit
- Copies of student Self-Evaluation
- Student I-Search Journal (Focus on Figures 3-21, 7-5, and 7-6)

Additional Activities

Description of Activity	Where does this activity need to be added?	Materials Needed	Person Responsible

Our National Heritage—This Land is Our Land Unit Resources

Information/Picture Books

Adler, David. 1994. *A Picture Book of Sojourner Truth.* New York: Holiday House.

Artell, Mike. 2001. *Petite Rouge: A Cajun Red Riding Hood.* New York: Dial Books.

Baylor, Byrd. 1982. *The Best Town in the World.* New York: Simon and Schuster.

Bolton, Janet. 1994. *My Grandmother's Patchwork Quilt: A Book and Pocketful of Patchwork Pieces.* New York: Delacorte Press.

Brown, Marc. 1991. *Arthur Meets the President.* New York: Little, Brown.

Burleigh, Robert. 1998. *Home Run: The Story of Babe Ruth.* San Diego, CA: Silver Whistle.

Castle, Caroline. 2000. *For Every Child: The UN Convention on the Rights of the Child in Words and Pictures.* New York: Phyllis Fogelman Books in association with UNICEF.

Coerr, Eleanor. 1986. *The Josephina Story Quilt.* New York: Harper & Row.

Coles, Robert. 1995. *The Story of Ruby Bridges.* New York: Scholastic.

Dorros, Arthur. 1991. *Abuela.* New York: Dutton Children's Books.

Flournoy, Valerie. 1985. *The Patchwork Quilt.* New York: Dial Books.

Freedman, Russell. 1980. *Immigrant Kids.* New York: Puffin Books.

Guthrie, Woody and Kathy Jakobsen. 1998. *This Land is Your Land.* Boston: Little, Brown.

Hayes, Joe. 2001. *Juan Verdades: The Man Who Couldn't Tell a Lie.* New York: Orchard Books.

Hopkinson, Deborah. 1993. *Sweet Clara and the Freedom Quilt.* New York: Knopf.

Johnston, Tony. 1985. *The Quilt Story.* Illustrated by Tomie dePaola. New York: Putnam.

Lowell, Susan. 1994. *The Tortoise and the Jackrabbit.* Flagstaff, AZ: Northland.

McKissack, Patricia. 2001. *Goin' Someplace Special.* New York: Atheneum Books.

Mills, Lauren A. 1991. *The Rag Coat.* Boston: Little, Brown.

Parton, Dolly. 1994. *Coat of Many Colors.* New York: HarperCollins.

Ringgold, Faith. 1991. *Tar Beach.* New York: Crown.

Saint James, Synthia. 1998. *No Mirrors in My Nana's House.* New York: Harcourt Brace.

Small, David. 1992. *Ruby Mae Has Something to Say.* New York: Crown.

Smith, Cynthia Leitich. 2000. *Jingle Dancer.* New York: Morrow Junior Books.

Spier, Peter. 1980. *People.* New York: Doubleday.

Suarez-Rivas, Maite. 2000. *Latino Read-Aloud Stories.* New York: Black Dog & Leventhal.

Turner, Ann. *Sewing Quilts*. 1994. New York: Macmillan.

Woodruff, Elvira. 1999. *The Memory Coat*. New York: Scholastic Press.

Web Sites

Teacher/Librarian Sites

Flannagan, Debbie. "Web Search Strategies." 1999–2004) (13 April 2004) Available: www.learnwebskills.com/search/main.html.

Jerz, Dennis G. 1997–2003. "BibBuilder 1:3 (Free MLA-Style Bibliography Builder)." (24 February 2004) Available: http://jerz.setonhill.edu/writing/academic/bib_builder/index.html.

McKenzie, Jamie. 2000. *Beyond Technology: Questioning, Research and the Information Literate School*. Bettingham, WA: FNO Press. (http://questioning.org).

Rubistar. 2001, 2002, 2003. "Create Rubrics for Your Project-Based-Learning Activities." (24 February 2004) High Plains Regional Technology in Education Consortium. Available: http://rubistar.4teachers.org/index.php.

Teachnology. 2003. "Rubric, Rubrics, Teacher Rubric Makers." (20 May 2004) Teachnology, Inc. Available: www.teach-nology.com/web_tools/rubrics/.

Warlick, David. 2000–2002. "Rubric Builder." (24 February 2004) The Landmark Project. Available: www.landmark-project.com/classwebtools/rubric_builder.php.

Yahooligans (citation examples for each grade level) www.yahooligans.com/tg/citation.html

Search Engines for Kids

ALA Great Sites for Kids (www.ala.org/greatsites)

Ask Jeeves for Kids (www.ajkids.com)

KidsClick! (http://sunsite.berkeley.edu/KidsClick!/)

TekMom's (www.tekmom.com/search/)

Yaholligans! (www.yahooligans.com/)

Clustering Search Engine (Teacher/LMS should bookmark research sites for students on school equipment.)

Vivisimo (http://vivisimo.com)

Picture Sites

Geo-Images Project (http://geoimages.berkeley.edu/GeoImages.html)

Library of Congress, America's Story from America's Library, "Come Celebrate" (www.americaslibrary.gov/cgi-bin/page.cgi/jp/celebrate)

Smithsonian American Art Museum (http://americanart.si.edu/index2.cfm)

Web site based on the book *On the Trail of the Immigrant,* by Edward A. Stiner (www.digitalhistory.uh.edu/photo_album/photo_album.html)

Folklore Sites

American Folklore: American folktales grouped by state and region (www.americanfolklore.net/rr.html)

American Folklore: Famous Characters at American Folklore (www.americanfolklore.net/ff.html)

America's Story from America's Library, Library of Congress, "Jackie Robinson Breaks Color Barrier" (www.americaslibrary.gov/egi-bin/page.cgi/jb/bball/Jackie_1)

____. "Quilts Today" (www.americaslibrary.gov/cgi-bin/page.cgi/jp/quilt/today_1)

AOL@School Elementary, "Quilts" (www.aolatschool.com/elementary/search/search.adp)

County and State Fairs (www.americaslibrary.gov/cgi-bin/page.cgi/jp/celebrate/fair_1)

Gallery of Vintage Quilts, "Vintage Gallery: Collection of Mary Babcock" (http://www.womenfolk.com/grandmothers/gallery.htm)

Geography World, "American Culture" (http://members.aol.com/bowermanb/amerc.html)

KIDPROJ'S Multi-Cultural Calendar, KIDLINK Society (www.kidlink.org/KIDPROJ/MCC/main.html)

KidsClick! "Quilts" (http://sunsite.berkeley.edu/cgi-bin/searchkids.pl?keywords=quilts&searchtype=all)

"Quilts as Symbol in America" (http://xroards.virginia.edu/~UG97/quilt/cult.html)

Quilt Books FAQs, "Children's Quilting Books" (www.ttsw.com/FAQS/BooksChildrenFAQ.html)

"Ramblin Round: The Life and Times of Woody Guthrie" (http://memory.loc.gov/ammem/wwghtml/wwgessay.html)

Sojourner Truth (www.sojournertruth.org and www.nationalgeographic.com)

Vivisimo.com Clustering search on quilts and Southern slaves includes African American, Underground Railroad, quilt history, Southern plantations, and Hidden in Plain View

Vivisimo.com Clustering search on regional folklore includes regional folktales, American folklore, weather lore, Mexican American folklore, folk and traditional arts

World Wide Quilting Page, "Quilt Blocks by Type" (http://ttsw.com/QuiltBlocksPage.html)

Videos

"All the Colors of the Earth." 1997. Weston Woods. (8 min.)

"Dancing with the Indians." 1993. Live Oak Media. (8 min.)

"Heritage of the Black West." 1995. National Geographic Society Educational Services. (25 min.)

"Jackie Robinson." 1992. Schlessinger Video Productions. (30 min.)

"People." 1995. New York: Lightyear Entertainment. (54 min.)

"Quilt." 1997. National Film Board of Canada. (6 min. 40 sec.)

"This Land Is Your Land." 2002. WEA Corp.

"Ty's One Man Band." 1989. Reading Rainbow. (30 min.)

"Victor." 1989. Milestone Productions/Barr Films. (27 min.)

Professional Books

Blecher-Sall, Hope, Catherine Waddington, and Merry Law. 2001. *A Travel Guide Through Children's Literature.* Fort Atkinson, WI: Alleyside Press.

Buzzeo, Toni, and Jane Kurtz. 2002. *35 Best Books for Teaching U.S. Regions.* New York: Scholastic Professional Books.

Day, Frances Ann. 1994. *Multicultural Voices in Contemporary Literature: A Resource for Teachers.* Portsmouth, NH: Heinemann.

Gibson, Karen. 2002. *Crash, Bang, Boom: Exploring Literary Devices through Children's Literature.* Fort Atkinson, WI: UpstartBooks.

Hall, Susan. 1990. *Using Picture Storybooks to Teach Literary Devices: Recommended Books for Children and Young Adults.* Phoenix, AZ: Oryx Press.

James, Helen Foster. 1996. *Across the Generations: Selecting & Using Intergenerational Resources.* Fort Atkinson, WI: Highsmith Press.

Kay, Heidi, and Karen DelVecchio. 2002. *The World at Your Fingertips: Learning Research and Internet Skills.* Fort Atkinson, WI: UpstartBooks.

Krech, Bob. 2002. *Best-Ever Activities for Grades 2–3: Listening & Speaking.* New York: Scholastic Professional Books.

Marantz, Sylvia, and Kenneth Marantz. 1994. *Multicultural Picture Books: Art for Understanding Others.* Worthington, OH: Linworth.

Moran, Karen A. 1999. *Literature Online: Reading & Internet Activities for Libraries & Schools.* Fort Atkinson, WI: Alleyside Press.

Polette, Nancy. 2000. *Celebrating the Coretta Scott King Awards: 101 Ideas & Activities.* Fort Atkinson, WI. Alleyside Press.

Semenza, Jenny Lynne. 2001. *The Librarian's Quick Guide to Internet Resources.* 2nd ed. 2001. Fort Atkinson, WI: UpstartBooks.

Stein, Barbara L., Gary Treadway, and Lauralee Ingram. 1998. *Finding and Using Educational Videos: A How-to-Do-It Manual for Librarians.* New York: Neal-Schuman.

Story-Huffman, Ru. 2002. *Caldecott on the Net: Reading & Internet Activities.* 2nd ed. Fort Atkinson, WI: UpstartBooks.

Story-Huffman, Ru. 2002. *Storybook Seasons on the Net: Reading and Internet Activities.* Fort Atkinson, WI: UpstartBooks.

York, Sherry. 2002. *Picture Books by Latino Writers: A Guide for Librarians, Teachers, Parents, and Students.* Worthington, OH: Linworth.

Standards and Textbooks

American Association of School Librarians and Association for Educational Communication and Technology. 1998. *Information Power: Building Partnerships for Learning.* Chicago: American Library Association.

Buckley, Susan, ed. 1997. *We the People: Explore Texas.* Boston: Houghton Mifflin.

Kendall, John S., and Robert J. Marzano. 2000. *Content Knowledge: A Compendium of Standards and Benchmarks for K–12 Education.* 4th ed. Aurora, CO: McREL. (18 August 2003). Available: www.mcrel.org./standards-benchmarks.

D POWERPOINT PRESENTATION

I-Search for Success:

Connecting the I-Search Process with Standards, Assessment, and Evidence-Based Practice

1

Department of Education mandates that all children be successful by 2014!

2

Department of Labor reports students' need to be information literate to succeed in the work world!

3

Parents want their children to succeed in school and have a rewarding career!

4

Students want to be heard.

5

"Allow us to tell you what we are thinking or feeling. Whether our voices are big or small; whether we whisper or shout it, or paint, draw, mime, or sign it—listen to us and hear what we say."

-For Every Child-
by Caroline Castle

6

How can these demands be met?

7

Consider brain research!

8

Our Brains

- Make sense of the environment
- Extract important information
- Look for relationships

—Robert Sylwester

9

Research Strategies organize this process!

10

The I-Search Process

- **Increases curiosity**
- **Aids in achievement**
- **Builds communities of lifelong learners**

11

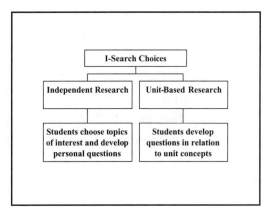

12

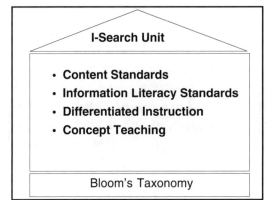

13

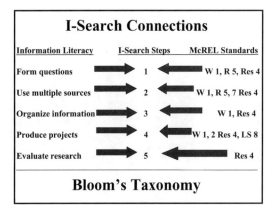

14

I-Search Action Plan

- What do we want to know?
- Where can we find the information?
- How will we understand and record the information we find?
- How will we show what we learned?
- How will we know we did a good job?

15

Why ask questions?

- Things change
- New information is created
- Yesterday's solutions won't work

—Jamie McKenzie

16

"The scientific mind does not so much provide the right answers as ask the right questions."

—Claude Levi-Strauss

17

Question!
What do we want to know?

18

Standards-Based Questions

This Land is Our Land Fourth Grade Unit

McREL History Standard Six Concept Cultural contributions from different regions help form the national heritage

Student Question Which region and cultural contribution of that region interests me?

19

"Good researchers research with a purpose. They search for answers to questions they have."

—Joyce and Tallman

20

Lessons

- Lesson 1: Introduce the Unit
- Lesson 2: Develop the Questions
- Lesson 3: Develop I-Search Action Plan

21

"Through the process of sorting out what they already know about their topic, students are forced to call up their knowledge and recognize their thoughts and connections about it."

—Robin Fogarty

22

KWR CHART

K What I know	W What I want to know	R My research questions
Old clothes	Slave quilts	How did the slaves in the South use quilts as maps? Why?
Pretty cloth	Maps	
Different designs	Decorations	What are some famous Southern quilt patterns and designs?
Cutout shapes	Patterns	
Cover beds	Designs	How do people in the South use quilts? Why?
	Family keepsakes	

23

Asking Questions

- There is more thinking and learning in asking questions than in answering them.
- Teachers ask 80 questions per hour and students ask two.

—Nancy Johnson

24

Explore!
Where can we find the information?

25

"If we strive to teach students the best way to critically evaluate the information that they find in relation to the purpose at hand, we will produce a generation of digitally literate adults who are equipped to learn throughout their lifetimes."

—Kathy Schrock

26

Lessons

- Lesson 4: Establish Careful Reader Strategies
- Lesson 5: Incorporate Context Clues and Vocabulary Development
- Lesson 6: Key Word Search
- Lesson 7: Reciprocal Teaching
- Lesson 8: Interview Experts

27

Resources

- **Periodicals/newspapers**
- **Brochures/pamphlets**
- **Information books**
- **Reference books**
- **Videos, CD-ROMs, DVDs**
- **Online databases**
- **Web sites**

28

Interview Experts

- Invite experts on the unit topic to class to be interviewed by students.
- Students find experts and interview them outside of class.

29

Create!
How will we understand and record the information?

30

Lessons

- Lesson 9: Take notes and Cite Sources
- Lesson 10: Differentiate Between Fact and Opinion
- Lesson 11: Evaluate Web Site Authenticity
- Lesson 12: Develop Research Skills
- Lesson 13: Summarize Notes

31

"These steps begin after students have defined and narrowed the task, constructed researchable questions, and located appropriate sources."
—Barbara Jansen

32

Note Sheet	
Name _____ Topic _____	
Question_____	
Notes p.	Source
Notes p.	Source
Summary	

33

Figure 5.5

Search Log

Date _____
What have I done so far?_____
_____
How have I done?
_____
What do I need to do next?
_____
Date _____
What have I done so far?
_____
How have I done?
_____
What do I need to do next?
_____

34

"The treasure word activity helped the students' summarization skills. They were practicing the skill in a meaningful format."

—Stephanie Smith, third grade teacher

35

Present!
How will we show what we learned?

36

Lessons

- Lesson 14: Construct Summary Boards
- Lesson 15: Draw Conclusions
- Lesson 16: Develop Main Idea
- Lesson 17: List Sources
- Lesson 18: Summarize the Search
- Lesson 19: Organize Writing Workshop
- Lesson 20: Produce Products, Make Presentations and Create Celebrations

37

"Encouraging students to write about topics that matter to them is probably the first step in helping students care about their writing."

—Calkins and Harwayne

38

The I-Search Paper

- Based on inquiry process
- Moves away from restating old information
- Allows for researching areas of personal interest
- Provides opportunity to express personality and voice

—Ken Macrorie

39

WRITING PROCESS

STEPS

first draft

revise

edit

peer conference

revise/edit

final copy

40

Presenting I-Search Projects

"Demonstrations and performances require communication skills which are necessary for success in the work force of today and in the future."

— Nancy Nagel

41

I-Search Projects

- Poster
- Diorama
- Mobile
- Puppet show
- Song/rap
- Big book
- Model
- Multimedia projects

42

Unit Celebrations!

43

Judge!
How will we know we did a good job?

44

I-Search Unit Assessments

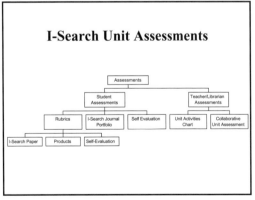

45

Standards-Based Grade Sheet											
Activity	R1	R2	R3	R4	W1	W2	W3	W4	W5	W6	avg
Literature activities		100									100
Interest map	98										98
KWL chart			95								95
Research planner			100								100
Search log			100	100							100
Note sheets	95		95	100		100					98
Summary board	95		100	95		95		98	98	100	97
Paper					100	98	96	100	95	98	96
Product			100								100

46

Students and the I-Search Experience

· I feel like I did an amazing job!
· The thing I liked most about this project was the research.
· When I was finished I felt relieved. I had a lot of fun!

47

"The I-Search project promoted cooperation not only between the teachers and the librarian but, also, among the students as they shared their research with one another!"

—Beth Stone, Elementary Librarian

48

What is success?

49

Success is

· Insuring that students achieve on state standardized tests.
· Preparing students for the next grade level, high school, and college.
· Laying a foundation for the world of work.
· Giving students a voice in what they learn and what they want to be!

50

Collaboratively, teachers, librarians, administrators, and parents can help all students succeed!

51

REFERENCE LIST

Abilock, Debbie. 1996–2003. "Information Literacy: Search Strategies." (24 February 2004) Available: www.noodletools.com/debbie/literacies/information/5locate/adviceengine.html.

———. 1996–2002. "MLA Bibliographic Format." NoodleTools. (24 February 2004) Available: www.noodletools.com/quickcite/cit-book.html.

Adler, David. 1994. *A Picture of Sojourner Truth*. New York: Holiday House.

American Association of School Librarians and Association for Educational Communications and Technology. 1998. *Information Power: Building Partnerships for Learning*. Chicago: American Library Association.

Amrein, Audrey L., and David C. Berliner. 2003. "The Effects of High-Stakes Testing on Student Motivation and Learning." *Educational Leadership*. Washington, D.C.: Association for Supervision and Curriculum Development (February): 32–37.

AOL@School. n.d. "Jackie Robinson." (20 April 2004) Available: www.harcourtschool.com/activity/biographies/robinson/.

Armstrong, Thomas. 1994. *Multiple Intelligences in the Classroom*. Alexandria, VA: Association for Supervision and Curriculum Development.

Blecher-Sall, Hope, Catherine Waddington, and Merry Law. 2001. *A Travel Guide Through Children's Literature*. Fort Atkinson, WI: Alleyside Press.Benson, Barbara P. 2003. *How to Meet Standards, Motivate Students, and Still Enjoy Teaching!* Thousand Oaks, CA: Corwin Press.

Berry, Kristin H. 1998. "Alien Annual Plants and the Desert Tortoise," Desert Tortoise Preserve Committee. (30 April 2004) Available: www.tortoise-tracks.org/publications/weeds.html.

Bloom, Benjamin S., ed. 1984. *Taxonomy of Educational Objectives: The Classification of Educational Goals*. New York: Longman.

Boruch, Robert F. 1997. *Randomized Experiments for Planning and Evaluation: A Practical Guide*. Thousand Oaks, CA: Sage.

Boynton, Alice, and Wiley Blevins. 2004. *Teaching Students to Read Non-Fiction Grades 2–4*. New York: Scholastic.

Brandt, Ron. 2000. "On Teaching Brains to Think: A Conversation with Robert Sylwester." *Educational Leadership*. Association for Supervision and Curriculum Development (April): 72–75.

Brooks, Jacqueline Grennon and Martin G. Brooks. 1999. *In Search of Understanding: The Case for Constructivist Classrooms*. Alexandria, VA: Association for Supervision and Curriculum Development.

Brown, Marc. 1991. *Arthur Meets the President*. New York: Little, Brown.

Burke, Kay. 1994. *The Mindful School: How to Assess Authentic Learning*. Arlington Heights, IL: IRI/Skylight Training and Publishing.

Caddell, Amy. 2002. "Tackle the TAKS." *Association of Texas Professional Educators News* (Fall): 23–27.

Calkins, Lucy McCormick, and Shelley Harwayne. 1987. *The Writing Workshop: A World of Difference*. Portsmouth, NH: Heinemann.

Carr, Judy F., and Douglas E. Harris. 2001. *Succeeding with Standards: Linking Curriculum, Assessment, and Action Planning*. Alexandria, VA: Association for Supervision and Curriculum Development.

Castle, Caroline. 2001. *For Every Child: The UN Convention on the Rights of the Child in Words and Pictures*. New York: Phyllis Fogelman Books in association with UNICEF.

Chapman, Carolyn. 1993. *If the Shoe Fits…How to Develop Multiple Intelligences in the Classroom*. Arlington Heights, IL: IRI/SkyLight.

Coalition for Evidence-Based Policy. 2002. "Bringing Evidence-Driven Progress to Education: A Recommended Strategy for the U.S. Department of Education." (November) (29 October 2002) Available: www.excelgov.org/displayContent.asp?NewsItemid=4548+Keyword=prppcEvide.

Coles, Robert. 1995. *The Story of Ruby Bridges*. New York: Scholastic.

Council for Excellence in Government. 2002. "Coalition for Evidence-Based Policy." Washington, D.C. (November). Available: www.excelgov.org/displayContent.asp?NewsItemid=4543+Keyword=prppcEvide (29 October 2003).

Development and Dissemination Schools Initiative. n.d. "Action Research Websites." (27 March 2004) Available: www.alliance.brown.edu/dnd/ar_websites.shtml.

Dodge, Robert. 2003. "No Child Left Behind Leaves Schools in Lurch." *Dallas Morning News*, October 5, 2003, sec. A.

Dorros, Arthur. 1991. *Abuela*. New York: Dutton Children's Books.

Drapeau, Patti. 1998. *Great Teaching with Graphic Organizers: Lessons and Fun-Shaped Templates that Motivate Kids of All Learning Styles*. New York: Scholastic Professional Books.

Duke, Nell K. 2004. "The Case for Informational Text." *Educational Leadership*. Association for Supervision and Curriculum Development (March): 40–44.

Duke, Nell K., and V. Susan Bennett-Armistead. 2003. *Reading and Writing Informational Text in the Primary Grades: Research-Based Practices*. New York: Scholastic.

Duncan, Donna, and Laura Lockhart. 2000. *I-Search, You Search, We all Learn to Research: A How-To-Do-It Manual for Teaching Elementary School Students to Solve Information Problems*. New York: Neal-Schuman.

Education Development Center, Inc. 2000. "Make It Happen—The I-Search Unit." (16 May 2004) Available: www.edc.org/FSC/MIH/I-search.html.

Elbow, Peter. 1981. *Writing with Power*. New York: Oxford University Press.

Flanagan, Debbie. 1999–2004. "Web Search Strategies." (13 April 2004) Available: www.learnwebskills.com/search/main.html.

Flournoy, Valerie. 1985. *The Patchwork Quilt*. New York: Dial Books.

Fogarty, Robin. 1994. *The Mindful School: How to Teach for Metacognitive Reflection*. Palatine, IL: IRI/Skylight Training and Publishing.

Gandal, Matthew, and Jennifer Vranek. 2001. "Standards: Here Today, Here Tomorrow." *Educational Leadership* (September): 6–13.

Gardner, Howard. 1983. *Frames of Mind*. New York: Basic Books.

Gibbs, Jeanne. 2001. *Tribes: A New Way of Learning and Being Together*. Windsor, CA: Center Source Systems.

Goleman, Daniel. 1995. *Emotional Intelligence*. New York: Bantam Books.

Graves, Donald H. 1994. *A Fresh Look at Writing*. Portsmouth, NH: Heinemann.

Guthrie, Woody, and Kathy Jakobsen. 1998. *This Land is Your Land*. Boston: Little, Brown.

Harrison, Crayton. 2004. "Less-Traveled Road." *Dallas Morning News,* May 11, 2004, sec. D.

Hattie, J. A. 1992. "Measuring the Effects of Schooling." *Australian Journal of Education* 36, no. 1: 5–13.

Heide, Anne, and Dale Henderson. 2001. *Active Learning in the Digital Age Classroom*. Portsmouth, NH: Heinemann.

Irwin-DeVitis, Linda, Karen Bromley, and Marcia Modlo. 1999. *50 Graphic Organizers for Reading, Writing & More: Reproducible Templates, Student Samples, and Easy Strategies to Support Every Learner*. New York: Scholastic Professional Books.

Jansen, Barbara A. 2003. "Reading for Information: The Trash-N-Treasure Method of Teaching Note-Taking (Grades 3–12.)" *The*

Big 6: Information Literacy for the Information Age. (12 April 2004) Available: www.big6.com/showarticle.php?id=45.

Jerz, Dennis G. 1997–2003. "BibBuilder 1:3 (Free MLA-Style Bibliography Builder)." (24 February 2004) Available: http://jerz.setonhill.edu/writing/academic/bib_builder/index.html.

Johnson, Doug. 2000. "Can School Media Programs Help Raise Standardized Test Scores?" *Knowledge Quest* 3, no. 3 (September): 27–29.

Johnson, Doug. 2004. "Plagiarism-Proofing Assignments." *Phi Delta Kappan* (March): 549–552.

Joyce, Marilyn Z., and Julie I. Tallman. 1997. *Making the Writing and Research Connection with the I-Search Process.* New York: Neal-Schuman.

Johnson, Nancy. 1995. *Active Questioning: Questioning Still Makes the Difference.* Dayton, OH: Pieces of Learning.

Kay, Heidi, and Karen DelVecchio. 2002. *The World at Your Fingertips: Learning Research and Internet Skills.* Fort Atkinson, WI: Upstart Books.

Kendall, John S., and Robert J. Marzano. 2000. *Content Knowledge: A Compendium of Standards and Benchmarks for K–12 Education.* 3rd ed. Aurora, CO: Mid-continent Regional Educational Laboratory. (18 August 2003) Available: www.mcrel.org/standards-benchmarks.

Kids Click. n.d. "Jackie Robinson." (20 April 2004) Available: http://library.thinkquest.org/10320/Robinson.htm.

Knickelbine, Scott. 2003. "The Money Hunt." *School Library Journal* (from *Curriculum Connections*) (October): 12–14.

Krech, Bob. 2002. *Listening and Speaking: Activities for Grades 2–3.* New York: Scholastic Professional Books.

Kuhlthau, Carol C. 2004. *Seeking Meaning: A Process Approach to Library and Information Services.* 2nd ed. Westport, CT: Libraries Unlimited.

Laase, Lois, and Joan Clemmons. 1998. *The Best Research Reports Ever.* New York: Scholastic Professional Books.

Lance, Keith Curry, Marcia J. Rodney, and Christine Hamilton-Pennell. "How School Librarians Help Kids Achieve Standards: The Second Colorado Study." Library Research Service, Colorado State Library, and Colorado Department of Education. (April, 2000) (19 May 2004) Available: www.lrs.org.

Langhorne, Mary Jo. 1998. *Developing an Information Literacy Program K–12: A How-to-Do-It Manual and CD-ROM Package.* New York: Neal-Schuman.

Lazear, David. 1998. *The Rubrics Way: Using Multiple Intelligences to Assess Understanding.* Tucson, AZ: Zephyr Press.

———. 1999. *Multiple Intelligence Approaches to Assessment: Solving the Assessment Conundrum*. Tucson, AZ: Zephyr Press.

Leigh, Jamie. n.d. "Quilts as Symbol in America." American Studies Program, University of Virginia. (20 May 2004) Available: http://xroads.Virginia.edu/~UG97/quilt/cult.html.

Levy, Steve. 2004. "All Eyes on Google." *Newsweek* 143, no.13 (March 29): 49–58.

Lewin, Larry. 2001. *Using the Internet to Strengthen Curriculum*. Alexandria, VA: Association for Supervision and Curriculum Development.

Loertscher, David L. 2000. *Taxonomies of the School Library Media Program*. 2nd ed. San Jose, CA: Hi Willow Research & Publishing.

———. 2003. "Project Achievement." Salt Lake City, UT: Hi Willow Research & Publishing. (9 February 2004) Available: www.davidvl.org/Achieve/achieve.html.

Macrorie, Ken. 1980. *Telling Writing*. 3rd ed. Rochelle Park, NJ: Hayden Book Company.

———. 1988. *The I-Search Paper*. Rev. ed. Portsmouth, NH: Boynton/Cook.

Martin, Robert S. 2002. "The White House Conference on School Libraries: Proceedings—Tuesday, June 4, 2002." Suppl. to *Knowledge Quest,* (Sept./Oct.): 1–93.

Marzano, Robert J. 2000. *Transforming Classroom Grading*. Alexandria, VA: Association for Supervision and Curriculum Development.

———. 2003. "ASCD Tutorials." Alexandria, VA: Association for Supervision and Curriculum Development. (January 2003) (20 January 2003)Available: http://webserver2.ascd.org/tutorials/standards/ques1.html.

Marzano, Robert J., Jennifer S. Norford, Diane E. Paynter, Debra J. Pickering, and Barbara B. Gaddy. 2001. *A Handbook for Classroom Instruction that Works*. Alexandria, VA: Association for Supervision and Curriculum Development.

Marzano, Robert J., Debra J. Pickering, and Jane E. Pollock. 2001. *Classroom Instruction that Works: Research-Based Strategies for Increasing Student Achievement*. Alexandria, VA: Association for Supervision and Curriculum Development.

McKenzie, Jamie. 2000. *Beyond Technology: Questioning, Research and the Information Literate School*. Bettingham, WA: FNO Press.

McKissack, Patricia. 2001. *Goin' Someplace Special*. New York: Atheneum Books.

Merrilees, Cindy, and Pamela Haack. 1998. *Ten Ways to Become a Better Reader*. Middleburg, FL: All Clay Printing.

Moore, David W., Sharon Arthur Moore, Patricia M. Cunningham, and James W. Cunningham. 1998. *Developing Readers and Writers in the Content Areas K–12*. 3rd ed. New York: Longman.

Mosteller, Frederick, and Robert Boruch, eds. 2002. *Evidence Matters: Randomized Trials in Education Research*. Washington, D.C.: Brookings Institution Press.

Nagel, Nancy G. 1996. *Learning Through Real-World Problem Solving: The Power of Integrative Teaching*. Thousand Oaks, CA: Corwin Press.

Naisbitt, John. 1982. *Megatrends: Ten New Directions Transforming Our Lives*. New York: Warner Books.

National Reading Panel. 2000. *Teaching Children to Read: An Evidence-Based Assessment of the Scientific Research Literature on Reading and its Implications for Reading Instruction*. Washington, D.C.: National Institute of Child Health and Human Development.

Northwest Regional Educational Laboratory. 2001. "6 + 1 Trait Writing Assessment Scoring Guide." (20 May 2004) Available: www.nwrel.org/assessment/scoring.asp?odelay=3&d=1.

NoteStar. 2000–2004. "Notestar: A Project Based Learning Research Tool." University of Kansas: ALTEC. (24 February 2004) Available: http://notestar.4teachers.org/.

Oberg, D. 2001. "Demonstrating that School Libraries Improve Student Achievement." *Access* 15(2): 15–17.

Palincsar, A. S., A. L. Brown. 1984. "Reciprocal Teaching of Comprehension Fostering and Monitoring Activities." *Cognition and Instruction* 1: 117–175.

Popham, W. James. 2001. "Teaching to the Test?" *Educational Leadership*. Association for Supervision and Curriculum Development (March): 16–20.

Price, Hugh B. 2002. *Achievement Matters: Getting Your Child the Best Education Possible*. New York: Kensington.

Quindlen, Terrey Hatcher. 2003. "Drawing out the Best." *Education Update*. Association for Supervision and Curriculum Development 45, no. 4 (June): 1.

Quinn, Quality. 2001. "The Principal: Closing the Gap and Getting Results." *Leaders of Learners* (May): 1–9.

Rogers, Spence, Jim Ludington, and Shari Graham. 1998. *Motivation & Learning: A Teacher's Guide to Building Excitement for Learning & Igniting the Drive for Quality*. Evergreen, CO: Peak Learning Systems.

Rubistar. 2001, 2002, 2003. "Create Rubrics for Your Project-Based-Learning Activities." High Plains Regional Technology in Education Consortium. (24 February 2004) Available: http://rubistar.4teachers.org/index.php.

Ryan, Jenny, and Steph Capra. 2001. *Information Literacy Toolkit: Grades 7 and Up*. Chicago: American Library Association.

Sagor, Richard. 1993. *How to Conduct Collaborative Action Research*. Alexandria, VA: Association for Supervision and Curriculum Development.

Schneider, Joan S. 1996. "The Desert Tortoise and Early Peoples of the Western Deserts." Desert Tortoise Preserve Committee. (30 April 2004) Available: www.tortoise-tracks.org/publications/schneider.html.

Schrock, Kathy. 2002. "The ABCs of Web Site Evaluation." 2nd ed. *Classroom Connect* (December 1998/January 1999).

———. 1995–2004. "Teacher Helpers: Critical Evaluation Information." DiscoverySchool.com: Kathy Schrock's Guide for Educators. (6 March 2004) Available: http://school.discovery.com/schrockguide/eval.html.

———. 1995–2004. "Teacher Helpers: Assessment & Rubric Information." Discovery School.com: Kathy Schrock's Guide for Educators. (6 March 2004) Available: http://school.discovery.com/schrockguide/assess.html.

Schrock, Kathy, Mary Watkins, and Jan Wahlers. 2000. *Writing and Research on the Computer*. Westminister, CA: Teacher Created Materials.

Semenza, Jenny Lynne. 2001. *The Librarian's Quick Guide to Internet Resources*. 2nd ed. Fort Atkinson, WI: Upstart Books.

Silver, Harvey F., Richard W. Strong, and Matthew Perini. 2001. *Tools for Promoting Active, In-Depth Learning*. 2nd ed. Woodbridge, NJ: Thoughtful Education Press.

Slavin, Robert E. 2003. "A Reader's Guide to Scientifically Based Research." *Educational Leadership* (February): 12–16.

Slavin, Robert E., Olatokunbo S. Fashola. 1998. *Show Me the Evidence! Proven and Promising Programs for America's Schools*. Thousand Oaks, CA: Corwin Press.

Small, David. 1992. *Ruby Mae Has Something to Say*. New York: Crown.

Smith, Cynthia Leitich. 2000. *Jingle Dancer*. New York: Morrow Junior Books.

Spandel, Vicki. 2001. *Creating Writers: Through 6-Trait Writing Assessment and Instruction*. 3rd ed. New York: Longman.

Spier, Peter. 1980. *People*. New York: Doubleday.

Sylwester, Robert. 2000. *A Biological Brain in a Cultural Classroom: Applying Biological Research to Classroom Management*. Thousand Oaks, CA: Corwin Press.

Teachnology. 2003. "Rubric, Rubrics, Teacher Rubric Makers." Teachnology, Inc. (20 May 2004) Available: www.teach-nology.com/web_tools/rubrics/.

Texas Administrative Code. 2004. "School Library Programs: Standards and Guidelines for Texas." Texas State Library and Archives Commission. (19 April 2004) Available: www.tsl.state.tx.us/ld/schoollibs/standards2004.html.

Texas Education Agency. 2003. *TAKS Study Guide: Grade 3 Reading and Mathematics.* Austin: Texas.

Todd, Ross J. 2001. "A Sustainable Future for Teacher-Librarians: Inquiry Learning, Actions and Evidence." *Orana* 37, no. 3 (November): 10–20. Eric Database. OCLC (30 October 2003).

———. 2003. "Irrefutable Evidence: How to Prove You Boost Student Achievement." *School Library Journal.* (April): 52–54.

Tomlinson, Carol Ann and Caroline Cunningham Edison. 2003. *Differentiation in Practice: A Resource Guide of Differentiating Curriculum.* Alexandria, VA: Association for Supervision and Curriculum Development.

Tomlinson, Carol Ann and Susan Demirsky Allan. 2000. *Leadership for Differentiating Schools & Classrooms.* Alexandria, VA: Association for Supervision and Curriculum Development.

Tomlinson, Carol Ann. 1999. *The Differentiated Classroom: Responding to the Needs of all Learners.* Alexandria, VA: Association for Supervision and Curriculum Development.

———. 2000. "Reconcilable Differences? Standards-Based Teaching and Differentiation." *Educational Leadership.* Association for Supervision and Curriculum Development (September): 6–11.

———. 2001a. "Grading for Success." *Educational Leadership.* Association for Supervision and Curriculum Development (March): 12–15.

———. 2001b. *How to Differentiate Instruction in Mixed-Ability Classrooms.* 2nd ed. Alexandria, VA: Association for Supervision and Curriculum Development.

U.S. Department of Education. 2002. "Education Department, Coalition for Evidence-Based Policy to Collaborate on New Initiative." (29 October 2003) Available: www.ed.gov/new/pressreleases/2002/04/04242002ahtml.

U.S. Department of Education Institute of Education Sciences National Center for Education Evaluation and Regional Assistance. 2003. "Identifying and Implementing Educational Practices? Supported by Rigorous Evidence: A User Friendly Guide." (10 February 2004) Available: www.excelgov.org.evidence.

U.S. Department of Education. 2002. "Report of Scientifically Based Research Supported by U.S. Department of Education." (30

December 2002) Available: www.ed.gov/Press Releases/ 11-20021182002b.html.

U.S. Department of Labor. 1992. The Secretary's Commission on Achieving Necessary Skills. "Learning a Living: A Blueprint for High Performance, A SCANS Report for America 2000." Available: http://wdr.doleta.gov/SCANS/lal/LAL.HTM (8 November 2003).

Utah Lesson Plans. 1997. "Centennial: A Patchwork Quilt. People of Utah." Utah Education Network. (17 September 2003) Available: www.uen.org/Lessonplan/preview?LPid+1034.

Vandervelde, Joan. 2001–2004. "PowerPoint Rubric." (5 May 2004) Available: www.uwstout.edu/soe/profdev/pptrubric.html.

Von Oech, Roger. 1986. *A Kick in the Seat of the Pants: Using Your Explorer, Artist, Judge & Warrior to be More Creative*. New York: Harper Perennial.

Warlick, David. 2000–2002. "Rubric Builder." The Landmark Project. (24 February 2004) Available: www.landmark-project.com/ classwebtools/rubric_builder.php.

Whitehurst, Grover J. "Evidence-Based Education." Office of Educational Research and Improvement: United States Department of Education. (20 January 2004) Available: www.gov/print/adminis/tchrqual/evidence/whitehurst.html.

Wiggins, Grant, and Jay McTighe. 1998. *Understanding by Design*. Alexandria, VA: Association for Supervision and Curriculum Development.

Winebrenner, Susan. 1996. *Teaching Kids with Learning Difficulties in the Regular Classroom: Strategies and Techniques Every Teacher Can Use to Challenge and Motivate Struggling Students*. Minneapolis, MN: Free Spirit.

Yahoo, Inc. 2002. "Yahooligans Teacher's Guide: Citation Sources." (5 May 2004) Available: http://yahooligans.yahoo.com/tg/678.html.

Zemmelman, Harvey, and Arthur Hyde Daniels. 1998. *Best Practice: New Standards for Teaching and Learning in America's Schools*. 2nd ed. Portsmouth, NH: Heinemann.

INDEX

ABOUT THE AUTHORS

DONNA DUNCAN

Donna has recently retired as Director of Library Services for Mesquite Independent School District. She is currently researching, writing, and consulting. Prior to being a director, she was an elementary teacher and junior high librarian in rural, suburban, and urban school districts in North Texas. She is a past chair of the Texas Association of School Library Administrators and she cochaired the Teaching and Learning Sub-Committee for the Texas School Library Standards. She is married to Bob; has two daughters, Laura and Lisa; two grandchildren, Mallory and Duncan; and two dogs, Max and Barney.

LAURA LOCKHART

Laura is principal of Hidden Lakes Elementary in Keller Independent School District near Fort Worth, Texas. She has taught third, fourth, and fifth grades and served as a reading and curriculum specialist and an assistant principal in a variety of school districts throughout Texas. She also presents workshops on I-Searching, brain-based learning and the reading/writing process. She is married to Jordon. They have a daughter, Mallory, and a son, Duncan.